1

3
6

4

FIELDS OF YOUNG CORN

Other writing by Anne Garnett:

The Cockstride (a play, published by Performance)
'Diary of a Somerset Housewife' (extract from her World War II diaries included in Michael Moynihan's anthology *People at War: 1939–1945*
Caught from Time. A Country Diary of the 1920s

FIELDS OF YOUNG CORN

Being the continuation of

CAUGHT FROM TIME

A Country diary of the 1920s

by

Anne Garnett

With drawings and paintings by the Author

TABB HOUSE
Padstow Cornwall

First published 1989

Tabb House, 7 Church Street, Padstow, Cornwall, PL28 8BG

Permission to reproduce photographs in this book
is gratefully acknowledged

Cover illustration by Anne Garnett

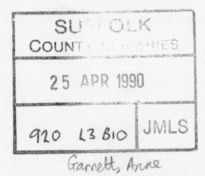
Typeset by St George Typesetting, Redruth, Cornwall

Printed in Great Britain by T.J. Press (Padstow) Ltd, Padstow, Cornwall.

CONTENTS

THE JOURNAL

LIST OF PLATES

Colour Pictures

Photographs

PRINCIPAL CHARACTERS

Agnes Victoria Sangar (AVS)	Anne's governess
Rex Sangar	AVS's nephew
Winifred Foster	A charge of AVS
Helen Marsden	A school friend
St John Couch	A friend; son of a vicar of Bicknoller

Family

Robert Garnett	Father. A London solicitor with literary interests. Eldest son of Richard Garnett, Keeper of Printed Books at the British Museum
Martha Garnett (Matty)	Mother. A novelist
Rayne Nickalls	Married sister
Narney Garnett	Eldest sister. Nurse at the Radcliffe Infirmary, Oxford
Richard and Robert Garnett	Brothers
Edward and Arthur Garnett	Uncles, Edward being the father of David Garnett, the novelist
Olive Garnett, May Hall and Lucy Cowlishaw	Aunts
Elizabeth Cowlishaw	Anne's cousin, daughter of Lucy

FOREWORD

*F*IELDS OF YOUNG CORN opens when Anne Garnett, the author, was lodging at Manor Farm with her governess Agnes Sangar (AVS). Anne had been sent by her parents to live in the country at the age of fourteen for her health, and had gone to West Somerset where AVS's father had been rector at Elworthy. Now, after several years of schooling at Minehead and several changes of lodgings, she had been informed by her parents that it was time to go back to London. This would mean for AVS the end of what had been the main interest in her life for many years, a roof over her head, and an income. The thought of returning to city life filled Anne with gloom, but she did not allow it to interfere with her interests. These included horses, her impending matriculation exams, painting, and observing and recording both in paint and words the world around her.

Fields of Young Corn is the conclusion of the diary Anne started in 1925 at the age of sixteen and kept for two years. The first part, *Caught from Time*, was put into print in 1986. After an interval of a few years the author was encouraged to prepare this volume. At the end of November, 1988, she spent a satisfactory week working on it with her younger daughter, the publisher of the two books, and within a month of that time on December 28th Anne died. During the last few days of her life, when someone remarked that she had always had a great gift for enjoying life, she replied "Yes, and I hope I have passed it on". *Caught from Time* enabled her do so, to a circle beyond her family and friends, and it is to be hoped that *Fields of Young Corn* will give equal pleasure, not only to those who remember the world she wrote of, but also to those who care to see those far-off days through her eyes.

CHAPTER I

June 1st — July 24th, 1926

❦❦❦❦❦ ❦❦❦❦❦

JUNE 1st. Today I had an invitation from Dorothy Dalzell, Mrs Dalzell's niece; her parents have taken a house at Crowcombe, so I started to walk there with racquet and shoes.

On the way I was overtaken by a trap driven by a handsome, black-haired woman — Mrs Waterman. Her younger daughter Frances was beside her. They recognised me and pulled up to shake hands; I walked along beside them.

My particular friend among the schoolchildren at Elworthy — apart from Edith — was Cissy Waterman but as we had read recently in the local paper that poor Cissy had been given nine months imprisonment for stealing a ring from her employer, I naturally did not mention her. However, Mrs Waterman, beaming with pride, soon said "Wasn't it bad luck about Cissy?" and I learnt all the details of the theft. They turned off at Heddon Oak, and soon after it began to rain.

I sheltered under a tree, but the rain went on so long that I gave up all hope of tennis and of getting to Crowcombe. I had an umbrella and made a tent for myself and a parcel of my tennis shoes to sit on, and was warm and dry. In the open spaces between the trees the rain fell like silver ribbons; mist-wreaths went cruising up among the greenery. There was a smell of wet moss; the woods were silent but for one pigeon cooing and a cuckoo calling now and then. Afterwards, when the rain stopped, numbers of little birds came out from their shelter; I watched them running up the tree trunks and fluttering in the branches.

AVS has been to see Miss Benison about my education, and as trains are so irregular they have decided I must spend another week as a boarder [at Minehead].

June 8th. I enjoyed Capt. Brandling's drawing lesson today at Minehead. For once he was encouraging, and told me I should try for a place at Lucy Kemp Welsh's School of Painting at Bushey. She has taken over from Herkomer and specialises in animals, especially

3

Cottage at Heddon Oak

horses. I think it a most helpful suggestion — and if we find a cottage for AVS I could still spend the holidays here.

This evening at school after tennis, we had permission to dance, and cleared the dining room. We put on Winifred Foster's gramophone, and at the end she gave us a dancing display. She is a good dancer and I enjoyed it; she wore a full-skirted white frock with a tight bodice that showed off her figure, and is so light one can hardly hear her feet. While she danced her eyes shone and her lips grew as red as paint. She is as proud of herself as a little peacock and somehow this adds to the charm.

June 14th. I finished all my work during the afternoon at school and came thankfully home to a clear evening. Just as well for as AVS and I were leaving for a walk with my sketching things, along came Mr Sweet Escott on Swallow. "Hullo — what a pity I didn't bring a horse for you, Anne, you could have come with me," — and then "Tell you what — look here, can you ride down to Vellow Wood and ask the farmer a simple question for me?" I ran to change and he asked AVS for a chair till I got back. There was some dispute over the boundary between Hartrow Estate and Preston Farm and he thought the farmer at Vellow, who used to be at Preston, would know what was right.

So off I trotted, Swallow seeming very broad and high after the ponies. She was a lovely ride, responding to every touch. The sun was sinking, and each moment the light grew more golden; I rode along between hedges of wild roses, honeysuckle, and shady elms full of singing birds. Everything is summery now — buttercups having given place to rusty sorrel and moon daisies and the sheen of the

4

ripe grass seeds. The bluebells are over too, and the air laden with the sweetness of clover.

The farmer was at home, and explained about the boundary, so I trotted back with the information and Mr Sweet Escott was most grateful.

June 20th. I had planned to go to Elworthy, but decided on the bluebell wood instead. It was a queer day, hot, with low, leaden clouds. And it was almost horrible in the wood. I seemed to walk from one sickly smell to another; what light there was was filtered as if through thick green glass. The undergrowth was waist-high along the path, the trees netted with honeysuckle with its blossoms high above me and pale as wax. There weren't many flowers; pale weedy lychnis and a few ghostly marsh-orchis. Further on under the beeches where the bluebells had been were masses of foxgloves in bloom, but pale too; it was pretty there, all pink and green. Then I came to the sombre, awe-inspiring part of the wood, where hollies and large fir trees grow; it was very dark. At last I came to the gap into the hayfield and was thankful to get into daylight away from the gloom and parasitic plants. I felt I had been inside Nature, in the place where she makes her creatures.

Once in the lane, the gravel crunching under my feet and well-trimmed hedges on either side, I felt quite ordinary again.

We are growing anxious about finding a cottage, as AVS has had her application for a council one at Crowcombe refused. So she was very pleased to have a letter today from Mrs Headlam, saying they would fetch us to look at 'the little house we told you of, at the bottom of our moor'. They had told us of it — it is for sale for £1,500 and they are fearful that undesirables may buy it. If AVS would be their tenant they think of buying it themselves.

A letter has also come from Narney asking if AVS would take her friend's little girl Pamela for the summer holidays. That is splendid, as AVS was thinking she would have to look for a holiday post. If she has a cottage she thinks she could manage with paying guests and the guineas she now gets fairly often for her dialect articles in various newspapers. Also, Miss Benison has asked her to take Winifred Foster for the holidays. Better and better!

AVS

5

June 26th.   Today's excitements will last us for a month! I had a morning at Bicknoller, riding Filbert while the Captain schooled the ponies in turn. It was very hot and sweat streamed off us all — especially me by the time I had walked home. It only takes me five minutes longer than from Brewers Water.

Punctually at three Miss Cockeran, Mrs Headlam's niece, and a girl named Deal came to fetch us in a large Ford car. The house in question is very nice; I made a discreet tour of it while AVS and Mrs Headlam were in deep conversation. But it needs a great deal of decoration and is in rather a sad state. There is also an empty bungalow — I wondered which was destined for AVS. Then I heard Mrs Headlam say "If I can get my old servant and her mother to live in the bungalow, would you consider the house? Don't think I'm offering you a house — I wouldn't presume on such a slight acquaintance — but it would be a help to me if you would come." Turning to me she added "Well, Miss Garnett, would you like to live here?" I was too delighted to reply.

June 27th.   Miss Smith (our Bridge player on the train) and I took our lunch onto Minehead beach today. We had it to ourselves at first, but then nurses and children came 'thick and fast, and more and more and more'. We were entertained by a faded little woman in charge of a plump, rather pretty little girl about eight years old. "Pixie darling, put on your hat and sand-shoes and play on the beach." This was repeated every few minutes, Pixie hopping on the pebbles with bare feet. Then an addition was made: "I shall be cross with you in a minute, mind!" At this Pixie sat on a stone and began to whine "I can't put on my shoes, I can't put on my shoes." After five minutes she varied this with "I want a drink. I want a drink." I was just about to throw a large pebble at her — which Miss Smith thought would be kind and effectual — when a diversion was caused by the faded guardian saying "I see Granny coming — run and meet Granny, Pixie."

Pixie's shoes were on in a flash and she dashed off. How my heart warmed to Granny! She was indeed a perfect dear, clad all in black and grey, with a black silk parasol. She took Pixie in hand at once, sending her off to make sand-pies, and sat down to talk to the ineffectual lady. We noticed her poking about with the parasol, and presently she remarked "Why, what a nice, *soft* stone! Come and look at it, Pixie — Why it isn't a stone at all — its a jelly-fish!"

Before we had stopped laughing at this, I heard a queer, rustling, creaky, padding sort of noise, and there emerged from behind our rock an extraordinary object about three feet high. It had bright plum-coloured lower portions, the upper being concealed by a huge lid of yellow straw. This object — very much like a large tropical beetle — slowly shuffled past, and raised a round fat face with immense dark eyes. It was a small boy in waders and straw hat. After him shuffled another, exactly similar, only a size larger. They were the oddest couple — Miss Smith christened them The Waddlers, exactly right. Altogether I found the people so diverting that I did not get much work done.

July 3rd. A message from Mrs Evans Smith came today, inviting AVS to lunch and polo. I had a ride in the morning and galloped Filbert on Woolston Moor; he bolted once and made off down the main road before I could pull him up.

There was the usual scramble to get the Captain ready for Polo but at last all was accomplished and we packed the ponies' rugs, bowls, the polo sticks, tea, and ourselves into the car. AVS sat in front and Mrs Evans Smith and myself in the dicky.

It was an exciting drive as we were late, and had to stop in Williton to have the tyres pumped up. Mrs Evans Smith had to work the horn — a thing that screams like a syren and which is worked by pulling a mysterious wire; she did it most conscientiously at every corner — they must have heard us in Minehead.

Polo was very good; we watched a fast match between Blues and Whites. Then a practice game in which the Captain played; the colt did well. Major Hanney had a nasty fall but was not hurt; his pony reared and toppled slowly backwards in a perfect curve. It fell on its shoulder and got up unhurt. I thought it must have broken its neck.

A letter has come from Rex asking AVS to find him lodgings here in August. This is disappointing as I shall be at Hardown; AVS wrote to tell him so and to suggest his coming from July 24th. I hope he will write soon and say yes.

We have found a good novel among the Baxter's *Saints' Rest*, Dr Blank's *Sermons* and *The Peep of Day* on Mrs Redd's shelves. It is by a young doctor named Somerset Maugham and is called *Liza of Lambeth*. I think it is very clever indeed.

July 13th. It is the first day of the exam [school certificate], for which I have to go to the art school in Taunton.

AVS came with me and we travelled with Miss Benison (my headmistress) who had thoughtfully brought a large drawing board, pens, knives, etc., that she thought I might need. We lunched at Deller's; I was greatly excited and nervous, dreading the spectacle of hundreds of boys and girls, and severe examiners.

I was therefore much surprised at finding the Art School completely deserted — one solitary youth was lounging about, looking at the pictures in a large studio. At last a hatchet-faced female bustled in: "Are you for painting? Well, hurry up, you're very late!" So I flew up to the cloak room for my paint-box, and for half an hour the youth and I sat, waiting.

At length a very fat man smoking an evil-smelling cigarette came and said we could start, and took us to another room where one orange and a blue thermos flask awaited us. We solemnly sat down to draw and paint this inspiring subject, in utter silence. The fat man came in from time to time, and at length remarked: "When you come to paint, remember the flask is supposed to be *black*"!

The hatchet-faced woman sat beside us, reading a book, and the Art School porter was making up accounts at a desk. Seeing me looking about for a clock, he very kindly lent me his watch.

We both finished at the same moment and complimented each other on our efforts. I then walked up to the park to meet Miss Benison. It was scorchingly hot, the air shimmered and danced, and the sun beat down on the hot, dusty street.

In the park Miss Benison was sitting bolt upright under her parasol; dirty babies sprawled around her on the parched grass and even dirtier children played ball and French cricket. Apart from the heat and stuffiness of Taunton I don't think I shall find these exams too dreadful.

July 15th. I had to rise early to catch the 8.10 train. Yesterday I had St John to cheer me on the journey, and we walked through Taunton discussing books. Today I went to the deserted park and sat on a seat all alone till 9.15.

There were swarms of boys at the Art School, humming like bees, and several girls today. Mr Barnicott, the stout gentleman, and his hatchet-faced sister both marched up and down to see that we did not cheat. It was terribly hot; the boys sat in their shirtsleeves and even Mr Barnicott removed his coat while his face grew more crimson than ever.

I caught the 1.45 train; it was very late starting. My nice engine driver, the young one, came along for conversation, beginning "Is it hot enough for you?" He continued about "the wife" and how his father had just retired from being huntsman to the South Dorset Foxhounds for sixty years. I was much interested, and asked him a great number of questions. Driving is cruel work this hot weather, he said, and moreover his was an old-fashioned engine which made the cab even hotter.

In the evening I finished *Liza of Lambeth*, sitting under our ash tree. It is tragic; I think Dr Maugham writes extremely well.

July 16th. Another grilling day. Taunton is suffocating. I can well understand Mr Browne's feelings when, pale and tired after a long day at Minehead, he used to say "I quite *dread* going back to Taunton, I really do."

It was a near-disaster for me too, as I did not take my paint-box for 'Design'. the hatchet-faced lady asked me where it was, and her face fell quite three yards at my reply. She thought I *might* pass if I shaded my design very cleverly, "But they make a great point of colour".

Sick at heart, I began work and then a brilliant idea occurred. I held up my hand, and when Miss Barnicott came, said "I suppose you couldn't borrow some paints from one of the art students?"

"Well, I thought of that, but I'm afraid they have all gone home — however, I'll see."

She went to the porter, who so kindly lent me his watch, and he went out, soon returning with a quite nice paint-box. He is a dear! He came in one morning as I was looking at some etchings on the walls, and asked if I was fond of painting. So I told him; he sighed and said "Oh, it's good to love it, isn't it?"

I had supper at Deller's, where the band — two violins, a piano and some potted palms — was playing. As I went in someone called "Miss Garnett" and there was Miss Barnicott! She had told me I would not need paints tomorrow, and finding herself mistaken, had chased after me on a bicycle. So she must have a good heart!

July 21st. An easier day; for one thing it is cooler. We had a pleasant composition paper in the morning, and after lunch (Deller's again) the boy I met on the first day was once again alone with me for figure-drawing.

Molly Tapper and her brother Oliver arrived this evening for a holiday; AVS has found them lodgings in Stogumber. They came round to see us this evening, and AVS told her funny stories. Molly for one shrieked with laughter, and smoked innumerable cigarettes.

July 23rd. It was the dreaded arithmetic paper today, at 9.30. We were only allowed ten minutes for each sum and they were frightful; I only managed five out of seven. On comparing notes with some girls afterwards I found all but one of my answers quite different from theirs.

Oliver very kindly met me at the station with his motor-bicycle in order that I might not be too tired for a walk. When we reached Manor Farm we found that Mrs Hunt and Pamela had arrived. Pamela is her granddaughter.

Pamela is a delightful little girl, five and a half years old, but tall for her age. She has smooth brown hair in a fringe, enormous brown eyes with long lashes, chubby rosy cheeks, and a tiny red mouth that curls up and up when she laughs, two dimples appearing in the fat cheeks.

Soon she went to bed, and Molly coming round, we walked to Monksilver. A field full of small pigs attracted Molly, who insisted on my helping to drive them around so that Oliver could take moving-pictures of them. As soon as we stopped, they stopped too, and insisted on chasing *us*! Oliver must have got some amusing shots.

We went as far as Combe Woods, which were lovely beyond description after Taunton and that Art School.

July 24th. The last day of exams. I bade Taunton adieu for six blissful weeks, and am not going to open another book till next term.

We celebrated my freedom with another lovely walk, past Brewers Water, Heddon Oak, Rexton Gorse and home by Lower Rexton and Hounds Hill Lane. It was actually raining at last, but pale sunshine gleamed and mist drifted across a sky of grey and silver clouds.

We sat for a long time on a gate in the woods, watching the slanting spears of the rain and a sudden rainbow. For once we seemed worthy of our surroundings, as we had an elevated conversation on theology. Having been dragged to church every Sunday of their childhood, Molly and Oliver detest conventional religion, and were amazed at my credulity.

Sitting on one of his waggons

10

Molly is fat, exuberant, and bursting with mirth. She has good features and a pink, cleverly made-up face with fair hair coiled round her ears. Oliver is different; a tall thin youth with spectacles, and very silent when they first came. He is twenty-one; I don't know if Molly is older or younger.

As we came home another halt was caused at Rexton Farm by two adorable puppies who wriggled out to greet us. The farmer was much amused at finding us sitting on one of his waggons, cuddling his puppies and being licked all over in the process.

CHAPTER II

July 25th — August 5th, 1926

❦❦❦❦ ❦❦❦❦

JULY 25th. Mrs Hunt is only staying a few days, to settle Pamela in; today she came with the Tappers and me to the Quantocks. We went by way of Kingston, Culverhayes, and Halsway Manor, which I have learnt was built by Cardinal Beaufort as a hunting-lodge for his niece Margaret. We climbed the combe behind the wonderful old house slowly, as we kept stopping to eat delicious whortleberries.

Up on top we came on the unexpected sight of *two cars* drawn up among the bushes. Imagine cars on the Quantocks! The track is only three feet wide and is full of deep holes and brambles, with knee-deep rifts of beech leaves in places. How could they have got there?

We climbed to the top of Will's Neck and gazed at the miles and miles of country at our feet. Then we had to descend the very steep, slippery path down to Triscombe. Mrs Hunt and Molly were much alarmed at such a precipice so Oliver and I went in front in case they slipped. We had a splendid cream-and-whortleberry-jam tea at the Blue Ball; Mrs Welch the landlady remembered Molly though she only saw her once, years ago, on a visit she and Imogen paid to us at Elworthy.

Oliver's silence quite vanished on the walk home; he talked a great deal of his work — building aeroplanes — and of how he enjoys flying at Stag Lane Aerodrome.* Mrs Hunt adds great zest to the party. How can I do justice to Molly, with her sparkling wit and peals of laughter? She is studying Drama in London and tells us of the students. One of the cleverest, and her friend, is a dark girl named Peggy Ashcroft. Molly thinks she has a great future.

Today has been jolly — such mirth, such feasting on whortleberries, such glorious views, and clumps of rustling heather. It was heaven after Taunton.

*His friendship with Anne was ended several years later, when he 'buzzed' Weacombe in a 'plane, and AVS wrote to tell him never to visit them again.

July 22nd. After a ride for me on Filbert in the morning we all spent the afternoon at Blue Anchor. I lunched with the Evans Smiths, who gave me a lift as far as Washford and from there I walked across the fields to the beach where I found everyone. The little Archer children were there with their nurse; they are staying with the new Dr Rogers and his wife at Stogumber.

Oliver gave the children rides over the sand in his side-car, the tide being as usual, miles out. Molly and I thought we would explore the rocks, and enjoyed paddling in the warm pools, but it was not so pleasant when we encountered patches of deep slimy mud. Coming back I heard a scream, and there was poor Molly, prostrate in a mud-bath! She laughed and laughed and was quite helpless; I had to pull her out before she sank from sight like Carver Doone.*

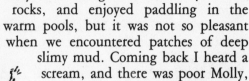

Oliver giving rides

Having washed off as much mud as we could, the Tappers returned on their motor-bike, the rest of us by train. Oliver met us at the station — he overflows with kindness and no trouble seems too much.

Having washed off as much mud as we could, the Tappers returned on their motor-bike, the rest of us by train. Oliver met us at the station — he overflows with kindness and no trouble seems too much.

July 28th. AVS and I went to tea with Mrs Headlam, her niece meeting us at Crowcombe Station. We went over Broad Oak Cottage again. It really is in a bad state, and the old lady is sensible in refusing the £1,800 that the owner now demands. We hope he will revert to the original £1,500, as he has had no other offers. We then walked to Mrs Headlam's own cottage and she unfolded her plans in case Broad Oak falls through. She always spends the winter abroad, and suggested that AVS should act as caretaker in her absence. It is a charming cottage, all nooks and crannies, latticed windows, and stairs opening from a cupboard as all cottage stairs should.

At tea the talk ran on a big fête at Crowcombe for which Mrs Sweet Escott has asked me for some sketches. Mrs Headlam has also been asked for some, and showed me hers. She asked to see mine, so I said I would bring them over. We offered Winifred's dancing as an

*A principal character in *Lorna Doone* by R. D. Blackmore.

13

added attraction; they seemed to think Mrs Trollope would be glad of her.

July 29th. We were all tired this evening after an even longer Quantock walk, to Holford, with tea at Bicknoller on the way back as we were all too exhausted to get to Stogumber. So we were glad when Winifred said she would dance for us. She put on her green tunic and floated round the room like a naiad; we encored again and again.

Molly and Oliver are most attracted; she is a lovely girl, slim and graceful and with red lips and grey eyes, "Put in with smutty fingers" as Molly said.

Record after record was put on the gramaphone: 'When You and I were Seventeen', 'Valencia', and 'Yearning'. Molly 'yearned' at the top of her powerful lungs.

July 30th. Winifred escorted me to Bicknoller on her cycle carrying my sketches, and I rode Filbert to Crowcombe in her company. He was lazy and we took nearly two hours. It was a beautiful day, very hot, but the ride was enjoyable through the green woods.

Miss Cockram kindly fetched us glasses of ginger-ale while my sketches were examined; we felt much refreshed and Filbert evidently was too; he trotted well and we did the seven or eight miles home in an hour.

We spent a lazy afternoon in the green tent formed by our weeping ash, Oliver playing with Pamela. She adores him and when bedtime comes, goes round kissing us all so that she can throw her arms around his neck; he gets three or four kisses and "I do love you, Oli*vier*".

To this pleasant group under the tree arrived Rex; a very pale, tired Rex, who hadn't much to say. Then Winifred danced, in her white floating frock, gliding in and out of the drooping boughs.

July 31st. Today Rex, Oliver, Molly, and I embarked on an ambitious expedition, to walk the coast from Porlock Weir to Lynton. We all met at Minehead, Rex and I having caught my friend the school train, and climbed into the Porlock 'bus.

Mr Wood and Keren got in soon after, sitting behind us. Mr Wood gave us much valuable information about our walk.

I have never seen the Weir so gay. The thatched cottages with their pink and white-washed walls were half smothered in flowers; roses, myrtles, and geraniums up to the roofs; huge blue and pink hydrangeas in the gardens. And at last we had the sea before us — for once clear and blue.

The little quay was crowded, 'buses constantly discharging their loads, but we were soon away and up the cliffs, on a path overhung with trees. A rest on a mossy bank was soon needed; lying there looking at the sea between the branches we stayed far too long and did not look like reaching Lynton.

At length we reached Culbone Church where of course we had to linger again, exclaiming at its tiny size and reading the John Ridds and James Shows on the gravestones.* Then it was a hot climb out of the woods to the bare fields, and once on top, scorching. But there was a marvellous view of the wooded cliffs sweeping abruptly down. Several rough fields led to a farm, and then a lane with delicious wild raspberries in the hedges. We then came to a high, bare field where we could see for miles, so had another pause, and one and all decided that it was far too late, and hot, for Lynton.

Back at Porlock — we sang all the way — it was discovered that Rex had lost our return 'bus tickets. Over a large tea at the Inn we devised a scheme to overcome this, as none of us had sufficient money.

It worked perfectly — Molly hunted in her bag and then said "Oh, I gave them to you, Oliver". Oliver, turning out his pockets, appealed to Rex, who then confessed to the conductor, with great charm: "I'm awfully sorry, I'm afraid we've lost them".

"Oh, that's all right, I'll trust you."

The 'bus ride was made memorable by a long argument about Roman Catholicism, which interested the rest of the occupants, even the driver joining in. Rex affirmed that the only true Christians are the Romans — all others being heretics. Oliver and I said "Nonsense" to this; Molly inclined to agree with Rex — but we had the driver on our side. We became quite heated; I was tired and sore by the time we reached Minehead.

Rex and I had a whole hour to wait for our train and a long delay before it started. Fortunately we had a carriage to ourselves; I was thankful to rest and watch a blood red sun sinking through an opaque, fiery sky.

At Watchet there was a real blaze — all the paper pulp on the quay had caught fire; two engines were trying to extinguish the flames.† The glare was reflected in the muddy harbour and the jets from the hoses turned into drops of blood. Behind it all the sunset glowed, another, steadier fire.

*More characters whose names were used in *Lorna Doone*.

†The import of esparto grass, timber and pulp for the paper trade was Watchet's chief industry.

August 2nd. I asked Rex if he would meet me on my way home after riding and Winifred said she would come too, to show him the way. I found them sitting on the bridge at Yard Farm, quite amicable; but they quarrelled all the way home, Rex teasing and Winifred attacking him like a little tigress. I find her quite good company when she is not rhapsodising about Miss Webster.

In the afternoon Rex and I set out for Elworthy, about two o'clock. We did not arrive till 6.00! We re-visited the little hut in Ashpier firwood that we found two years ago, and it was so delightful under a tree there that we lost all sense of time.

We visited Mrs Ware first. She was very pleased to see us, but I could tell at once that there was something wrong. Presently she said "You'll have heard the bad news, Miss Anne?" Her niece, a girl of twenty-one, who has just got a BA at Bristol, was killed by a tractor at Norton. She was walking on the grass at the side of the road when it ran into her.

At Whites Farm Mrs Hayes' tongue clacked with news. Rex made intelligent noises now and then and I put in "How dreadful!" and "Never!" where I thought fit. The best story was that the Landers are leaving the old Rectory and so far have not sold it. Miss Lander and the parson have quarrelled and he has not been up to say goodbye. An organ recital was given, a duet being played on the old harmonium and the new pipe organ recently installed. Miss Lander, who has played every Sunday for two years, was not asked to perform. Worse, she was not even told that her services were not required — she went over to the Church to find a complete stranger seated at her organ! I cannot think how or why Mr MacTaggart can have been so obtuse.

By and by Ned came in for a splendid tea, and then took us round the farm. Before leaving we visited the church with Mrs Hayes, to see the new organ. It is most imposing, but it is queer to see it in that little church.

Mrs Hayes came with us halfway up Mondsborough and Mrs Ware looked from her door to bid us goodbye — Dear people!

Walking back we built castles in the air. Rex would win the Calcutta Sweep and buy the old Rectory; I would re-model the stables and keep horses. It was so fascinating planning all this that we could hardly bear to reach Manor Farm.

August 3rd. This afternoon Molly, Oliver, Rex and I picnicked in Combe Sydenham woods. We sat by the big pond for our tea, gazing into the calm water and being bitten to death by midges. Then we began to tell funny stories; they grew more and more funny till on the way home it became necessary to separate. The boys fell to the

In the woods

rear to tell their stories, then Oliver came up and repeated them to Molly, she in her turn imparting them to me. This eventually palling, we fell to singing songs.

We parted for supper, but met again under the tree to make plans for tomorrow. It is to be a Great Day — the Opening Meet of the Devon and Somerset Staghounds at Cloutsham, and I am to ride over with Mr Sweet Escott.

August 4th. I got up for an early breakfast shared with Oliver; he then took me up to Hartrow in his side-car. Mr Sweet Escott once again came out munching his breakfast, and I went to the stables to pat Peter and Swallow as they were being saddled up. Then a young cousin of the Escotts, Bickham I think, came out; he was to go back with Oliver and have my seat in the car.

We started about 8.30; it was a beautiful morning, clear and fresh. Dew still lay on the grass, the sky was a pale blue.

I have never enjoyed a ride more. We rode right over the Brendons and met but few people; a man cracking stones, and here and there a farmer on his shaggy pony. Where we could look through gaps in the beech hedges, we could see the view. A tremulous blue haze hung over the country, and the golden cornfields, fresh pastures, darker woods and the pale blue of the Channel all looked remotely vague. How can I describe the pleasure of the swinging trot, the little shivery twitch of muscle on Peter's shoulder, the beat of eight hoofs?

At Wheddon Cross we fell in with a possession of cars that lasted all the way up the long hill to Dunkery Gate. The air was thick with dust and it was a relief to press through the gate to the open moor. Heather and bracken crossed by narrow, stony tracks, swept up to the Beacon on our left, and fell sheer on our right to a wooded combe below. And below that stretched the whole world.

The sun was hotter now, but a fresh breeze came from the Channel, and a line of snowy clouds over the Welsh hills gave a promise of coolness later.

We crossed the hill slowly, passing many cars drawn up by the track, and at last came to where a patch of black, white, and pink showed the meet far below.

17

It was a very steep descent, and at every turn we met more people, and cars drawn up at the side of the precipice. We came to Webber's Post, where hundreds of men, women and children, cars, char-a-bancs, and motor cycles were drawn up in the heather, as no traffic was allowed further.

From here an easier hill led us down into the cool woods, and we were joined by whole companies of riders: ladies riding side-saddle in neat habits, girls astride, children on fat ponies, immaculate men with cream breeches and yellow waistcoats, and old gentlemen stiffly astride their quiet mounts.

We all trotted along the twisting road, the sun sifting down on us in speckles through the oaks; here and there we forded a stream with a mighty splash. Then up a steep path, past Cloutsham Farm, and pushing through a gateway, were all at once in the centre of the meet.

There was a crowd of abut 200 horsemen and countless foot-people; in the centre we could just see the pink coats of the hunt servants and get a glimpse of the pack. Peter was thrilled with it all; he bickered for joy and when I gave him the rein fairly danced, but he behaved beautifully. Bickham and Rex soon found us and came to talk. I felt so happy, sitting on eager Peter and talking to their up-turned faces.

At last there came a lull in the chatter, and the horn sounded, sending quivers through Peter and me. A stream of horses pressed through the gate; we waited for some time till we heard the tufters in the woods below. The horn spoke softly now and then; we trotted down past the farm till suddenly five or six horsemen clattered down a track and galloped past us. Peter grew so excited that I thought it best to let him out and we had a glorious gallop, our echoes clattering in the trees and ringing on the hillside. So we came up to Webber's Post, and drew rein among twenty or so horsemen.

The tufters were working the woods opposite, and towards Luccombe. After a rest we slowly climbed a steep track, and looking back saw the pack and a whole procession of horsemen going to replace the tufters.

At last we reached the top of the moor and with many others reined up to watch. Now and then a hound spoke and the horn blew. Mr Sweet Escott wanted to find the car for a drink, so we rode on, looking for Bustle's yellow car among all the hundreds. We went as far as Dunkery Gate, and there I left him as he was tired, and hacked back to search again. As luck would have it I rode into the entire field. A man in pink was shouting; I did not know if to me, but as I approached it became obvious; I rode up to him and he explained that he had been trying to hurry me up to him, to leave room for the stag to break. When I had apologised he told me where the tufters had found, and where the pack had been laid on. I rode on, looking for the car. Peter could not understand why I had left the others, and was very restless.

At long last I found Bustle, seated in an Essex car, not the Yellow Peril; he said he had just seen two stags cross the track, and that the rest of the party and gone off to the Beacon, taking all the food and drink with them.

I rode back with this sad news; Mr Sweet Escott had dismounted so I got off myself; we ate the sandwiches from our saddlebags heartily and felt more thirty than ever.

By this time the field had moved off to Codsmoors, and Mr Sweet Escott said we had better not follow as it would be too much for the horses. At that moment three fine stags came bounding down Dunkery and crossed the track quite close to us. Thrilling!

We rode slowly back to Wheddon Cross, where we reined up at the inn for very welcome drinks. There was a priceless fat old man there in an enormous car, complaining that he did not think much of this stag-hunting. "If it was foxhuntin, Sir — by George, Sir, I've done plenty of that in my time, but 'pon my soul, Sir, I don't see much sport in this. Where can I go to see a bit of sport?" As it was clear that wherever he went the car would go too, it was difficult to suggest a view-point.

Even though refreshed by our drinks, it was a relief to climb the long hill up from Wheddon Cross, where Peter went so slowly that I could take my feet from the irons and double them up to rest them on his withers.

The hack home did not seem too long, tired as we were, until the last three miles; they were the limit. We were too tired to talk and just plodded on. The white gate at the top of Hartrow drive was a most welcome sight.

In the yard at last we slithered off our horses, and Mr Sweet Escott, remarking "Well, I think I've been a *little* bit too far", stumped over the cobbles into the house.

I went upstairs to wash, and then down to the cool dining-room where everyone was at tea. Mrs Sweet Escott and the boys were anxious to hear our adventures; Bickham was already there, having returned with our party and cycled up on Winifred's bike. Tea was a blessed meal.

The new Swedish boy and Bickham were to play tennis at the Kershaws and drove me home in the pony-trap; at least, the Swede and I drove and Bickham tore down Ashpier on Winifred's bike. We found him on the lawn at Manor Farm with the bike upside down and the whole party trying to find the puncture he had made. Altogether I had ridden forty miles, and Mr Sweet Escott says that if I am not stiff tomorrow I am one off the Seven Wonders.

19

August 5th. AVS very sportingly brought me my breakfast in bed; when I got up I can honestly say I was not in the least bit stiff. The morning was spent in packing, as, alas, I go to Hardown tomorrow. However, Helen will be there, the Tappers are leaving too, and Rex will be travelling with me as far as Yeovil.

He and I went to watch Polo in the afternoon, by train. We had hoped for an empty carriage but they all seemed full, and when I appealed to Tommy, our porter, the horrid boy grinned from ear to ear and pushed us into one full of old ladies. Rex groaned as he sat down between a dame with an enormous basket and a spinster with a fox terrier, and asked "How long did you say this journey will take?"
We had to suffer for forty minutes; the windows were shut lest the fox terrier should leap out, and at Watchet several squirming babies were carried in by their mothers.

Polo at Dunster

He and I went to watch Polo in the afternoon, by train. We had hoped for an empty carriage but they all seemed full, and when I appealed to Tommy, our porter, the horrid boy grinned from ear to ear and pushed us into one full of old ladies. Rex groaned as he sat down between a dame with an enormous basket and a spinster with a fox terrier, and asked "How long did you say this journey will take?"
We had to suffer for forty minutes; the windows were shut lest the fox terrier should leap out, and at Watchet several squirming babies were carried in by their mothers.

At the polo ground we were hailed by Mrs Frost and invited to sit up on their hood. She took my hand, saying "I haven't seen you for an age", whereat Duddles exclaimed "Sh — be quiet! Traill is playing, — the Argentine — that's him with the sheepskin under his saddle". We were all perforce silent; Traill's play was certainly worth attention, and at the end of the chukka Mrs Frost was allowed to continue, and gave me full details of her recent operation.

When we reached Stogumber station, we found the Tappers, AVS, and Winifred catching our train for the Crowcombe fête, where Winifred was to dance. Rex and I continued home, to put Pamela to bed. After I had tucked her up she remembered that she had not said her prayers: "And I'm a bit shy of saying them to you." We overcame this difficulty and she added two hymns, sung in an

On the Quantocks, towards the Blackdown Hills

p.17. At Cloutsham, where 'we heard the tufters in the woods below'

Farmyard and domestic animals

2

Shadows skimming . . .

On the Quantocks

Chap.3. Lyme Regis from Stanton St Gabriels, Dorset.

5

Sept.11th. Le Nerrepot, a Brittany farmhouse

Binic. Aug.31st. 'Our cove this morning – a pearly-grey one'

Sept.4th. Near Binic, Brittany.

June, 1926. At Minehead

*The Bristol Channel
from East Quantoxhead*

*Bracken and the larches
at Weacombe*

extremely shrill voice. Her chief love is still Oliver, but Rex too has succumbed to her fascinations, and the other day spent a whole hour helping her to dress in flowers and leaves as a fairy.

I have enjoyed the last fortnight. Perhaps after the grilling two weeks of the exams any holiday would have been lovely, but this: the long walks over heather, the cool evenings sipping coffee and watching Winifred dance, and the uproarious songs and laughter! One evening Oliver climbed to the very top of the weeping ash, all Stogumber coming out to watch. We had just been discussing Darwin and Molly remarked "He's reverting to type". Winifred made us laugh too: we were lying under the tree, talking of Italians. "Italians!" said Winifred. "Ugh, nasty, oily creatures, you can't trust them — especially the men."

"But why?" we asked in astonishment. "Do you know any?"

"Oh, yes, I know them through and through — I've seen them on the pictures."

Molly gave me a description of Imogen's life in Rome one day, I think as we walked back from Bicknoller. She had been staying there herself, and thought poor Imogen was having a very difficult life between her mother, Signora Angeli, and married aunt, Signora Agresti. She is supposed to be studying Art, but does not have much chance, as she has to look after her mother who is ill. Unfortunately there is nothing Mrs Angeli hates more than being looked after; consequently Imogen gets sworn at in true Rossetti fashion all day long, and in the intervals her aunt swears at her for not being a dutiful daughter. Molly was with them for five months so knows all too well how difficult the situation is, and being a loyal friend, grew very heated about it. I was disturbed myself as I have always been fond of Imogen. She has a difficult temperament I know — our Miss Rossetti is the only tranquil member of the family.*

I slept with Winifred, to have a good night before the journey; Pamela does kick rather!† I have very mixed feelings about going away — it will be lovely at Hardown with Helen there, and I hope Uncle Arthur. Father's youngest sister Lucy Cowlishaw is coming with my cousins Margaret and Elizabeth. Uncle Arthur told me I should like Elizabeth; she is just my age but as they have lived in France since the war we only met as little girls. So I am looking forward to seeing them — but how I shall miss the happy life here!

*Imogen Angeli was the neice of 'our Miss Rossetti', Mary, a daughter of William Michael Rossetti and neice of Dante Gabriel Rossetti, the pre-Raphaelite painter and poet.
†At that date it was still common for women to share a bed; in the working classes children of both sexes did, while in the 19th century Anthony Trollope the novelist remarked that gentlemen would no longer consent to do so.

CHAPTER III

August 6th — August 27th, 1926

❧❀❧❀ ❀❧❀❧

A UGUST *6th.* We went early to 'the Tappery' to bid Molly and Oliver farewell and found them packing up the motor-cycle; they had a hearty send-off as they at last phut-phutted away. Then it was my turn to say goodbye to AVS, who looked very cut-up at our parting. Of course, I had the excitement of Hardown to look forward to.

Rex and I had an hour to wait in Taunton and walked into the town, thus breaking my vow at the end of the exam: "I won't enter this accursed place till next term".

We travelled to Yeovil with two old farmers, and tried to be cheerful. Yeovil is a vile town; it was raining and we felt impending disaster and gloom, as one does on a wet railway station. We could not find a nice place for lunch in the town, so returned to the platform buffet — dirty, gloomy, and horrid. Then Rex bought me a *Punch*; my train came puffing along; a last wave and I plunged into a tunnel. In an instant, Rex had vanished from my life and I settled down to my *Punch*, a horrid little ache in my heart.

I only had to change at Yeovil Junction and caught a Greybird 'bus to Morecombelake. The ride was nice, through Lyme Regis and Charmouth with the green hills like a frozen choppy sea and the coast with Golden Cap looming up.

I toiled up Hardown Hill to be greeted by Mother, and Father came up from the cottage for tea. Later, Mother and I went down to the Ship to meet Helen, but she was not on the 'bus. A moment later, she hopped out of a taxi as dainty and pretty as ever.

We strolled on the top of Hardown after supper, walking round and round on the short heather until the sunset faded and lights twinkled out at Lyme.

August 7th. Coming back from a bathe, a car drew up, containing the Tolleys. Basil jumped as if he had been shot when he saw Helen. Mrs Tolley had told her last summer "Yes, Helen, Basil likes you *very* much."

From Hardown Hill

Helen Black* and her friend Ursula Gregory arrived today. I remember 'Blackie' from the Grove School when she taught Art and could not keep us in order, and was agreeably surprised to find her so congenial here. She is amusing, brisk, and matter-of-fact like her mother but with a great deal of imagination. Ursula seems old-fashioned, her hair secured by a velvet band in a bun; she wears ample shirts of 'art fabric' with flowing scarves and beads. Her voice is as gentle as a sucking dove; she really coos, and I long to hear her shout just once.

August 8th.   Helen and I went to Whitchurch for Matins. Passing old Mrs Parkinson on the way, we said "How do you do?" and in the porch were the Tolleys, who greeted us warmly. No sooner were we in a pew than Mrs Parkinson came over to us and said in audible tones "How *do* you do, my dears? — I did not recognised you in the lane but, of course, I know who you are now — how are you?" She is evidently deaf, but I had to repeat my enquiry as to her health three times, to the interest and edification of the entire congregation.

Mrs Tolley, on leaving the church, murmured the magic words tennis and bathing-picnics. She looks as dashing as ever. Basil seemed shy, lowering his eyes or looking away whenever Helen turned in his direction.

We walked up the lane with Mrs Parkinson who invited us to tea in the afternoon to meet her great-niece Joy, who is our age and at the Godolphin School at Salisbury.

Having elected to go by the upper lane, longer than we expected, we arrived late and found the family at tea. The party consisted of the burly schoolmaster and his athletic wife whom we met last year,

*Niece of Constance Garnett (née Black), who was the translator of Russian novels, wife of Edward Garnett and mother of the novelist David Garnett.

23

our hostess, Joy's mother and Joy herself. She has dark shingled hair and wide blue eyes. Her mother was skilfully made up with a good-natured face and deep, husky voice; she kept me in a state of suppressed giggles by grinning at me over the table.

After tea we sat in the drawing-room and talked, or as it turned out, I talked. Everyone laughed at my stories, and joined in with anecdotes. I kept trying to stop and then someone would launch me off yet again; it made me uncomfortable.

August 9th.   We shopped for Mother in Bridport in the morning, the chief purchase being an enormous codfish that I had to carry like a baby. The fishmonger assured me that he would wrap it up to look like a bottle — it was a magnum at least!

In the afternoon we went to the top of Hardown to sketch. It was stormy, with inky clouds blotting the sunny view in torrents of rain. I tried to paint a storm on the coast while Helen did a sunny scene from the other side of the hill. It was difficult with the light changing but the storms looked so fine that I rushed as it in a sort of agony lest it should be a failure and a fever of haste to get my washes on before the rain fell.

August 10th.   We spent a foggy, damp day making sweets for Summer Tolley's stall at the Flower Show. We first made delicious toffee and stuck fruit jellies into it; peppermint creams and almond toffee. Then we tried barley sugar from a a recipe book dated 1786. This did not get on at all satisfactorily. It had to boil till 'cracking point'; we boiled it and boiled it and boiled it until we realised that we were at cracking point ourselves, and left it to go on alone on the kitchen range while we went to clean off our stickiness for dinner.

In the afternoon we cut up our sweets and poured the barley sugar to cool in a tin. It was then a lovely golden viscous syrup like Lyles' only far more delicious. If only it would set! By the evening it was hard enough to cut into shapes and we conceived the brilliant idea of making a complete alphabet.

August 11th.   Our first act was to visit our barley sugar. Alack! The beautiful alphabet was no more; in its place lay pools of syrup. It was a great blow, but we packed the other sweets into boxes and took them round to the Tolleys. "I know where you are going with those," shouted the Major as we came up with him in the lane. He called Summer and she showed us all she had collected for her stall and exhibits of vegetables. We saw Basil too, not quite so shy, for he actually talked to Helen. Both he and Summer have grown very tall.

August 12th. Our household was up early, as Mother was showing flowers and entries had to be in by 9.30. She had arranged six varieties of flowers in separate jars and very grand they looked.

Helen and I dressed ourselves in our best and went down to the show about three o'clock. The band was already playing, flags waved from the top of two marquees, children ran hither and thither, and ladies displayed their wares at the various stalls, attracting attention by ringing dinner bells.

A lady named Mrs Weston 'read characters' in a little tent at the top of the field. People had to consult her alone, so Helen went first and I followed. I felt fearfully nervous and, trying to be at ease, said brightly "You tell fortunes, I believe."

"No," said Mrs Weston, so severely and suddenly that I jumped, "I read characters."

I sat down and she took my hands; I learnt that I suffer from nervous headaches, am irritable and obstinate but — here she looked at my face severely — *truthful*. I had never travelled but would do so soon; had I the means I should be very extravagant and I shall marry twice, the second marriage being the happiest, and shall have three children.

This seemed to be all there was for 1/- so I departed. Helen had heard much the same but she is to have one very happy marriage.

Much to our joy, Mother was awarded a second prize for her flowers. After the prize-giving, we waited a long time for the tent to be cleared for dancing and when at last it was, sat on a bench with Basil, Joy, and Margaret MacGregory. Basil was noble and danced with each girl in turn but I think he enjoyed those with Joy the most. She dances divinely and has won a silver cup. I very much fear that she has cut Helen out.

The 'floor' being of much-trodden turf and with only one partner between the four of us, Helen and I did not stay long. "Going already?" cried Major Tolley and as we explained the absence of males, said with genuine feeling "How I wish I were younger!" The Tolleys have done most of the work for the show; there appears to have been a slight coolness with Mr Lee, as he resigned from the committee and though present, did nothing towards the arrangements.

August 13th. It was too foggy and cold to bathe today, so we decided to walk to Symondsbury as we did last year. The lane was not so interesting this time, as the bushy over-arching greenery had been cut. The restoration of the church was nearly complete and the inn as nice as before.

But the cider! I had three glasses and felt decidedly dizzy. Helen confessed to a feeling that one of her legs was shorter than the other.

We all rose from the table and with rigid faces crossed the room to test our sobriety, but it was a decided effort.

Going home, everyone pretended to be drunk. I think we were, a little. Blackie did it to perfection and was so funny that Father laughed until the tears came — whereupon we all pointed accusing fingers: "Ugh, he has reached the maudlin stage". My dizziness soon wore off, and Helen's legs resumed their correct proportions, but we kept up our display for some time.

Symondsbury

August 14th. We had a happy afternoon's tennis at the Tolleys; their court is good and we had some five sets; Helen and I played against Basil and John first and then Joy played with me against Helen and Summer with return matches after tea. Needless to say, Joy played very well and most gracefully.

When we got home, Aunt Olive had arrived, more tortoise-like than ever, even on land. We went to bed quite tired from the tennis but neither Helen nor I had much rest. I woke up feeling very ill and was at last violently sick and hearing unmistakeable sounds from Helen's room, tottered in to find the poor girl in the same dire state. We had a dreadful night — I swear I will never laugh at sea-sick stories again!

August 15th. Helen had recovered by the morning, but I still felt ill; I ate nothing and lay on the sofa, with a burning pain in my stomach. Everyone is mystified by our illness but I suspect the meat, which often has to be washed with Milton as it has begun to go off. It is very difficult to keep food fresh in the larder here; Mother is a great believer in the efficiency of Milton but I would much rather that she threw anything suspect away.

In the evening I felt better and Helen, Aunt Olive and I went to the service at Whitchurch. Evensong there is most eerie and the singing so faint that it sounds like a whisper among the huge round Norman columns. Mr Lee gloats and grimaces in the pulpit, the candles illuminating his bald head wobbling upon his skinny neck. He has a habit of crouching back in the shadows like a cat about to spring, or a spider watching a fly. His voice sinks to a whisper and then stops and you hear the clock in the tower: 'Tick-tock, tick-tock'. Basil was in the choir, and rather amused at finding himself there in a surplice, he grinned whenever he looked our way. We met the whole family after the service and were invited to a bathing picnic tomorrow.

August 16th.   In spite of fog, it was a jolly picnic, with twenty-two people including Edward Lee and his elder sister, Euphemia. After bathing we were given a stunning tea with all manner of cakes, buns and sandwiches laid out on a cloth. I sat with Joy and Helen at her adored Mrs Tolley's feet. We then played sardines — a failure — and hide and seek which went better. I was with Joy most of the time and Helen with Summer. Then we had a game of tip-and-run cricket in a field, the boys making terrific hits right to the beach.

Joy said she would walk home with us, but as we were leaving, Basil put his head out of the hut — the boys were having another bathe — to say "Hullo, Joy, I'll come with you if you'll wait a minute."

"Thanks awfully, but I'm going back with these two."

I thought both their faces fell, and felt it sad, so said hastily "That's all right Joy; you have your bike and will have to push it all the way if you come with us."

Joy replied that she was cross with Basil and that it would do him good! On the way home we spoke of the Tolleys and I noticed that she said very little about Basil but she defended him vehemently when I said something about sixteen being a silly age. For we have discovered that the adult-looking Basil is in reality only sixteen. Helen and I think that they are in the process of a romance, which interests us greatly.

The Cowlishaws had arrived in our absence. Uncle Arthur, as usual, is right; I know that I shall like Elizabeth, who has been staying with him at the Huts. She has black curly hair, grey eyes behind thick lensed spectacles, a beautiful mouth, slim graceful figure and a clear olive complexion.

Poor Margaret would be really lovely were she normal, but she has a pronounced thyroid growth and has not developed mentally. Mother told me that before she was born Aunt Lucy had to assist at Grandmamma's emergency operation [believed to be for a strangulated hernia] which took place on the kitchen table. Grandmamma only lived a few hours after it and it was thought that the shock accounted for Margaret's abnormality.

Aunt Lucy herself is a woman of large bulk, ponderous, and with an air of melancholy brooding. She has bulging blue eyes and a drooping mouth and stoops very much, but she is humorous and kindness itself. A life of struggle has made her so, added to the fact that she could never settle happily to one religion. First she was extremely high Church, then a Roman Catholic and is now, I believe, an atheist, having been (I imagine) disillusioned by French curés, and anyway by the fact that she knows life to be dust and ashes!

They are going on to Brittany from here and at supper Aunt Lucy said "We badly need a fourth in the party and hope perhaps you will trust Anne with us."

"Well, that would be delightful," said Mother, and Aunt Lucy went on to detail the trip, pointing out the low state of the franc, the cheapness of the hotel and the delights of the fishing village, Binic. She concluded with "So we do hope you'll come — do you think your Father will let you?"

"Well, I don't know," I said. "He wouldn't let me go to Scotland once when I had the chance." And no more was said.

August 18th. After breakfast, Aunt Lucy said that Father wished to see me in his study at the cottage. "About Brittany". However, when I arrived, full of expectation, he said it was about me. I received a grave lecture on my attitude to my elders. Father said that I appeared to regard them as queer beings, only half alive, who should be awakened, and pointed out the absurdity of this as their ways are now fixed and are on the whole very good ways.

Also, did I realise how I wounded him by my reference to Scotland, as if he were in the habit of docking my pleasures instead of indulging them as he does?

I listened patiently, and felt awfully sorry for my unfortunate remark about the Scottish invitation. I had known I was wrong the moment I made it. When he saw that I was really ashamed, he said that I might go with the Cowlishaws to Binic.

Hardown Cottage

But Father does annoy me. He is so selfish — it shows in little ways such as always letting us girls open gates and carry baskets. Once when I remonstrated, he groaned and said "You don't realise how I'm getting on in years." That is his line: "I've worked for you all these years, why aren't you grateful?" Of course, I am grateful but one does not want it rammed down one's throat.

At meal times this summer Father is very irritable. Naturally with this large party and the two aunts who don't often meet, we all talk

28

and, with so many women, often all at once. Everyone knows that Aunt Olive talks incessantly, at the top of her voice. Father groans and shuts his eyes and says "No, do let us be quiet. We'll have silence if you please." Elizabeth is splendid and once retaliated "Well, Uncle, our talk may not interest you but it does us — and I don't talk as much as you!"

In the night, when I think of leaving Somerset for this grumpy man I lie and cry. There will be nothing but books to console me at West Hill and I don't want to read about life, I want to live it!

My one attempt to persuade Father to allow me to stay on in Somerset and go to the Taunton Art School was a failure. His mind is made up. At Helen's suggestion I wrote to Dicky about it and had such a nice letter back but it offered no hope, only good advice.

I do feel it silly not to get on with one's parents. I do with Mother — usually I fail with her and do splendidly with Father. This time Mother is sympathetic and sweet and has not given me one lecture.

When I left the cottage the mist had dispersed and the sun was shining from a blue sky. So Helen, Elizabeth, and I decided to go to a Horse Show at Hawkchurch that we had seen advertised. Elizabeth and I cut sandwiches and Helen went down to the Post Office to send a wire to AVS about Britanny. I don't want to go without her approval as I had told her I would be returning on September 14th.

We missed our 'bus and halfway to Charmouth on the next, realised that we had left our lunch in the porch of the Ship. We asked to be put down at the nearest point to Hawkchurch; the conductor consulted the driver and returned to say that we should have a walk of five miles.

Feeling unequal to ten miles there and back, we got off at Lyme and bought some lunch and went onto the cliffs to eat it and laze away the afternoon. The rolls and potted meat tasted heavenly lying in the grass, the wind stirring our hair, and the blue sea below us. We lay on our backs staring into an intensely blue sky; the shadows of white clouds skimmed over us and along the coast, changing the cliffs from gold to grey and back to gold again.

The first hour was perfect but I began to feel ill and soon as sick as a dog, but without being sick, and so was faint and miserable. The others were most sympathetic but, of course, unable to help and after a while my agonies abated.

Cups of tea in Lyme Regis lost us another 'bus so we walked on the front picking out pretty girls. Helen and I have great eyes for this but we do not agree. "Do look at that SWEET girl."

"Sweet? My dear, I think her a fright. Now, there is an attractive one," and so on. This has led to so many controversies that I have begun to study Helen's taste and we agree better.

At last we caught a 'bus home, where everyone was astonished at our not going to Hawkchurch; they seem to have not expected us back until midnight! There was a telegram from AVS: 'Delighted'. So I can now look forward to Brittany; the character-reading lady's words are coming true already.

Helen and I now share a bedroom and in the night she became very ill, as I had on the cliffs, but she was soon quite sick and much eased, and felt better by dawn.

August 20th. A wet day, impossible for bathing, so Helen and I went to Bridport to have my passpost photograph taken. I have written to Dicky for an application form; there is not much time as we sail on Saturday week but we hope we may just do it.

The photography was an ordeal, the man treating us as naughty children. "Now, we might just as well do it properly — would you mind sitting over here? You are upsetting her," as Helen giggled. Of course, we missed our return 'bus; it would not be us had we caught it.

In the evening we were sitting round the fire sewing and reading when I heard something, and looking up beheld Uncle Arthur at the window. I flew to the door, hotly pursued by Elizabeth. It was lovely to kiss him again; of course in an instant he was surrounded by the whole party but I was the first.

August 21st. Another wet day. Uncle Arthur, Elizabeth and I saw Helen off in the morning and made a mournful little procession back to the house, the duller without her.

In the evening we had a surf-bathe in a very rough sea. Immense breakers were booming up, filling the air with spray, and a broad ray of sunlight came through the storm clouds to shine on the white horses. Elizabeth and I danced in the surf, pretending to be members of the Russian ballet, standing on one leg and then falling to let the waves cream over us.

August 22nd. Aunt Olive and I went to church and Mr Lee kindly signed my passport form in the vestry afterwards. Elizabeth, Margaret and I went to the top of Hardown to try to sketch the cloud shadows skimming over the blue-green country, while Margaret did her embroidery.

In the evening I bathed with Uncle Arthur and Elizabeth; there were fairly big waves and I felt a coward and would not go out far. The others went a long way beyond the breakers — Elizabeth swims like a fish.

August 24th. We all bathed today, except Mother and Margaret. It was calm and I swam a good deal, feeling envious of my cousin who went right out with Uncle Arthur and Father.

I had a sad letter from AVS, to say that after all, she is not having Broad Oak Cottage and is to look for a room in London. She thinks Broad Oak too risky from a financial point of view: I had not realised that so much depended on my boarding with her. Mrs Headlam kindly offered to rent it for her and see how she got on but, of course, it would not be worth buying furniture which would take her savings. I am very much against the idea of her living in London; she would be wretched and I should have no links with Somerset and not even holidays there.

I felt very unhappy about this, and the realisation of living at West Hill weighed on me. I told Uncle Arthur all about it and he was sympathetic and kind. He came over and gave me a good hug and kiss for which I loved him.

He has a habit of suddenly kissing; one day he was patting Elizabeth's back and she said, feeling cross at the moment, "Why do you keep patting me?"

He said "I'm not particularly anxious to," and I told him he could pat mine, as I liked it. I got several kisses instead. Yet he is the last man you would think would kiss anyone, so masculine, brown, and out-of-doors.

This afternoon the MacGregors gave a picnic at Charmouth. We all went in a very crowded 'bus, packed like sardines. Mr MacGregor was less angry than usual — he is generally like a bear with a sore head and snappy and rude to Margaret [his daughter]. Everything the poor girl does is wrong but she keeps her temper and does not answer back. How she controls herself I don't know: practice I suppose; she has plenty of that! She is remarkably sunny-natured considering the time she has.

We undressed in some reeds under the cliffs a little way up the beach and had a bathe. You can walk for miles at Charmouth before you are out of your depth and feeling secure, I swam quite a lot. More guests arrived for tea and we played ball before the party broke up.

As we were sitting down for supper, Uncle Arthur said "Anne, there's a young man on your track." I sprang to the front door and found Basil. "I've come at the last moment — we forgot all about you. Will you come down for games in the garden at eight o'clock?" It was then 8.00! I hurried through supper, flew to change and ran all the way.

A large party was assembled on the terrace — everyone save the Lees, playing the 'Who am I?' game. We all had famous

31

characters pinned to our backs and had to go round asking questions about ourselves until we discovered our identities. I had James II; very difficult. After this we went into the garden room to guess advertisements.

Joy and I sat on the low wall of the terrace for a delicious supper, brought to us by the boys, and then we played sardines. It was fearsome in the dark, searching all over the garden, inky shadows under the trees and shapes looming up. The moon had not yet risen but it was a clear, starry night.

Joy and I were the first to find the hidden sardines and so the next to hide, which we did by crouching in the kitchen garden between rows of beans and peas. It was the best possible place and no one found us for a long time. It was amusing to hear their comments as they searched.

The moon had risen over Golden Cap by the time we were released. We were both very dirty and I had a sore eye caused by an inquisitive gooseberry bush. Then we played hide and seek. Joy and I ran 'home' almost at once and walked about talking while the rest flitted by. I heard a great deal abut Basil — 'Bas Dar' as his fond mother calls him — and Joy's difficulties. She finds Mrs Tolley very jealous of her children and particularly of Bas Dar and though they are all kind to Joy she feels she is not approved of.

The party then broke up but as I left I heard Joy and Basil beseeching Mrs Tolley to get the car out for a moonlight bathe. She gave in and though I was urged to go with them I thought three bathes in one day, and all the games, rather too much. Aunt Olive and Uncle Arthur were waiting up for me and I was warmly applauded for my virture in coming home.

August 26th. Today was the day of the annual Whitchurch Grand Fête. Aunt Lucy thought she would save her energies for it and stayed at home with Margaret while the rest of us bathed at St Gabriels. Uncle Arthur, Elizabeth, and I were in front, and in the sea before Father and Aunt Olive arrived. While Elizabeth and I were sunbathing naked, Aunt Olive began to scream. We thought she must be drowning but her head and shoulders were out of water: she continued to emit short piercing cries like a seagull. Then we realised that two men were approaching and that her cries were to warn us. It was too late to do anything but pull our frocks over us; we lay still except for shaking with repressed laughter.

We then thought we would climb Golden Cap, a long-talked-of feat; and Uncle Arthur, Elizabeth, and I achieved it. It was very hot and though the climb did not take long it was a relief to fling ourselves down on the heather at the top after the 640 foot scramble. The only difficult part was the Golden Face at the end, almost sheer, but we found rabbit holes for our feet for most of it.

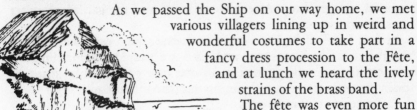

Golden Cap

As we passed the Ship on our way home, we met various villagers lining up in weird and wonderful costumes to take part in a fancy dress procession to the Fête, and at lunch we heard the lively strains of the brass band.

The fête was even more fun than last year. We went down about four o'clock and had a very good tea and then watched the sports. Major Tolley was one of the judges and his wife was soon talking away to uncle Arthur, obviously greatly taken with him, in common with all her sex.

The sports were worth seeing: tilting the bucket, high jumping, flat races, and a point-to-point over the brook and up the hill, hurdle and obstacle races and heaven knows what. John Tolley was the only entrant for the donkey race and looked absurd, jogging round on a diminitive donkey that refused to trot and laid its ears back and bucked when flogged. Elizabeth and John got on like wildfire and had not been introduced three minutes before they were ragging each other, squabbling and sparring. They crawled underneath the tarpaulin nailed down for the obstacle race; Uncle Arthur, Summer and I stole up and stood on the edges so that they were trapped.

We were much surprised to see Summer with a large coconut. "How did you get that?" asked her Mother.

"I bet you didn't knock that down for yourself," shouted John. Summer put her nose in the air and maintained a dignified silence, but confessed to me later that she had asked a man to win it for her.

Margaret MacGregor was anxious to go in for the three-legged race but neither Elizabeth nor I were good at it and all others failing, Uncle Arthur rashly said that he would be her partner. As Margaret came about up to his knees, they made an ill-assorted couple and fell down every two yards. However, they finished in fine style amid loud cheers.

Mrs Tolley had promised Mrs MacGregor that they would see Margaret home but as their car was full and she wished to leave early she asked me if Margaret could come with us. "Whatever you do, don't let her stay for the dancing; her mother does not want her to and she is wild to stay."

I duly told Margaret that we would take her home; she asked anxiously if we were staying and disagreed when I said I thought

33

there would only be villagers at the dance. She then disappeared and Summer and I spent a long time looking for her. Everyone we approached said "I haven't seen her for a while" or else "Her mother is anxious for her to be home early".

At last the Tolleys went off, Mrs Tolley's last words being "For heaven's sake get Margaret home! She is a naughty girl at times — gives people no end of trouble." After much further searching we finally unearthed her in a cottage at supper with a friend.

She gave us trouble too, saying she was sure her Mother would not mind her staying, so-and-so would see her home. She DID want to stay — please, please. All this with tears in her eyes and a pitious expression, that would have melted a heart of stone. We all tried to do our best, but even Uncle Arthur could not pursuade her so we had to leave without her, feeling very angry.

I was terrified of telling her parents. Suppose that her father should open the door? I should die of fright. Uncle Arthur pointed out "Hang it all, its nothing to do with us," and fortified by this and Elizabeth's support, we arrived at the cottage. Here we found Mother and Aunt Olive, come to say that Margaret was all right and coming with us.

It was very hard to tell my tale without making things black for Margaret. As it was, they came out pretty grey. Her mother was extremely annoyed — thank heaven, Mr MacGregor did not appear — and we heard a great deal about Margaret's solemn promise to return and the conditions under which she had been allowed to go in the first place. Poor Margaret! I pitied her home-coming. "Well, I've seen worse fusses over a dance before now," was Uncle Arthur's comment as we climbed up Hardown.

Garden at Hardown

August 27th. Today was spent in an agony of apprehension lest my passport should not come. It was not among the morning post and I became horribly worried. However, this wore off in the pleasure of my uncle's company. He and I bathed at St Gabriels. It was quite calm, the tiny waves breaking on the shore with a long-drawn sigh. Seagulls floating showed that there were fish about and we saw several small shoals of mackerel, quite close.

The postman came in the afternoon and I sorted the letters with trembling hands — Hurray! There was my passport! With a light heart I joined Mother and Aunt Olive to pick blackberries in the lane above our house, and hearing a shout, saw Aunt Lucy and Elizabeth coming up to learn if the passport had come.

For our last evening we had a very good game of Bridge.

CHAPTER IV

August 28th — September 20th, 1926

❧✿❧ ❧✿❧

AUGUST 28th. The great day at last! My parents and uncle gave us a hearty send-off, Aunt Olive coming with us in the 'bus as far as Lyme Regis and giving a wealth of good advice on parting. The train to Salisbury was crowded and we had the usual hour to wait there. I suggested going to the cathedral and was glad I did so, for it is glorious.

I loved the town too, with quaint narrow streets and bridges over the clear river where green weeds lift and wave. I loved the sunny close with fine old trees and mellow Georgian houses. But best of all was the cathedral with its wonderful spire.

The station was a nightmare after this. We waited half an hour on a crowded platform and it was insufferably hot. At last we reached Southampton and took a taxi to the docks where we left our luggage and arranged to meet at eight o'clock. For, feeling it a chance not to be missed, I had written to Mrs Sangar suggesting a visit and had a reply yesterday. I thought it likely that Rex might be there; in any case it would be lovely to see them.

So I boarded a Shirley tram and was soon walking up Anglesea Road in a great state of excitement. At my ring, Miss Smythe came running from the garden, followed by Mr Sangar, and his wife came downstairs to greet me even more warmly. They gave me a delicious tea and the cats, Frizzy and Snowdrop, were brought in to welcome me. Rex was expected at any moment from Switzerland! Mr Sangar kindly came with me to the docks, where we all met as arranged. There was a delay before we could go on board and we watched the sun set behind the cranes and tall masts in the dockyard.

Elizabeth and I explored every nook and cranny of the boats, but much to our chagrin Cooks had made a mistake and had not booked our berths. The Purser had small hope of our getting them, saying that he had seventy on the waiting list already and the boat-train had yet to come.

We enjoyed watching cars being loaded by a crane, like gigantic beetles swinging in mid-air, and the red and yellow lights reflected in the harbour, the hot smell of the engines and their throb and hum.

At last the boat-train came panting into the great shed alongside and hundreds of people swarmed up the gangways. I'd never dreamt of so many. Soon after — about 12.30 — we started to swing slowly round and Elizabeth and I flew to the Purser's office.

He called out various names to the twenty or so of us clustered round his little grating; at last came 'Cowlishaw' and we found we had two lovely white cabins between us.

Elizabeth and I shared, and I had the top bunk, with the moon shining in at the port-hole. We watched it glistening on the waves, and at last fell to sleep, but with the sucking and gurgling of the sea all too near for my peace of mind. It seemed impossible to feel safe with all that water beyond a plank or two.

About three o'clock I woke with terror — A MAN was crawling over me! It was only the steward come to screw up the porthole. We were now rolling a good deal, the waves breaking quite high. The Steward told us we were well out in the Channel and apologised for waking us; we heard his footsteps, and knocking, and "I'll just close that porthole, please" die away down the companion-way, and tried to sleep again. But the slap of waves and sounds of anguish all round kept us awake and at length even the much-travelled Elizabeth was sick.

August 29th.   I awoke to a blood-red sun rising through golden haze over blue sparkling waves. We both dressed and ran up on deck, at about 6.30. The dark blue sea water was full of racing white crests and there was a high exhilarating wind. We were just passing the Channel Islands, which lay like dim clouds on either side.

At 8 a.m. we descended for breakfast. I was hungry after the cold air and tackled bacon as well as rolls and coffee but Elizabeth could not eat much.

After 9 a.m. we sighted land and were soon sailing into a wide bay, dotted with islands, some of them fortified. Then came the crowds at the gangway, French porters and the customs and at last we were out in a broad sunny road under the massive city walls of St Malo.

Our train was not until 1.10 p.m. so we had the whole morning to see the town. An arch in the walls led to a very narrow street between tall houses, the church spire overlooking it all. Here we had our money changed; we needed a portmantau to carry the French cash!

The shops surprised me; they were a regular jumble of goods all huddled pell mell, not neatly arranged like English ones. The streets were crowded, everyone talking at the tops of their voices, and with no traffic at all save an occasional car crawling at a snail's pace and honking incessantly.

We saw Moors with lovely silk scarves for sale, soldiers in strange (to me) uniforms, sailors with red bobbles on their caps, funny little boys with long curls and Lord Fauntleroy suits, and women in deepest mourning with long crepe veils. I thought them all widows until Elizabeth explained that in France everyone goes into mourning for the death of any relative. All the time the bells rang, clocks struck, gramophones played, and dogs barked. Every now and then processions passed with drums and fifes, trumpets and horns, making more din than the whole British Army put together.

We bought bathing dresses and then went to a *perfumerie* to have our hair cut. We were shown up a long flight of wooden stairs and a little fat man appeared. "You will haf you 'air cut, n'est ce pas?" and before we knew it we were in chairs with sheets draped around us.

Another woman was having a trim, her husband looking on and conducting a conversation with the barber in rapid French. The barber would run a comb through my hair and then gesticulate with it wildly to this man, then take up the scissors and go off again.

After the couple left I did receive the benefit of his complete attention; he was sarcastic about the way the English had cut my hair. I explained that it had been cut by a friend (Helen) as we were in the country far from a shop. He said that it meant a great deal for the friendship that she was still a friend. He then became complimentary and observed that I was "as brown as a little bitch!" This disconcerted me a little till I realised that he meant 'peach'. I admired his tact with regard to Elizabeth, who was plainly longing to be shingled, but Aunt Lucy said "No".

"Oh, thees will not a single," said the little man, proceeding to shingle her curls. Aunt Lucy admired his artistry without realising what it had accomplished.

After this we went to an hotel by the city walls where a band was playing in the square and people were sitting at little tables all round, sipping wine. We had an excellent lunch of lobster mayonnaise and then made for the station. It was further than we thought, so we hailed one of the many ramshackle cabs that plied up and down with thin, weary-looking horses, and clambered in.

The rest of our journey seemed endless. The train crawled along between green fields, orchards and woods, where the trees were nearly all pollarded. We changed at little country stations all alike, with no platforms, where our train sauntered into dusty yards, people casually crossing under its nose. At one such place I saw a sight that will haunt me for the rest of my life. Two tall skinny beggars —

I suppose they were lunatics — were mopping and mowing at the edge of the station and had attracted a crowd. They had fluttering rags that showed terrible sores and scars all over their bodies. It was hard to tell their sex but I think one was a woman; the most horrible thing was that they had lost their hair in great patches. Their wild faces were dreadful and reminded me of the poor man in the tombs at Gadarene.

It was now very hot and we were tired and, oh, the smuts! We were black and gritty from head to foot. At last we reached St Brieuc and there took a little toy train like a row of trams strung together. It ran along the street, emitting fearful screams to warn the public strolling and standing on the lines. We grew too tired to care what happened and endured the many long halts and the chatting crowd of peasants returning from a fête quite placidly.

The whole train was packed with wrinkled old women in lace caps starched and wired into fantastic shapes, black serge dresses and little woollen shawls. Their children were mostly blue-eyed and sturdy and uncomfortable in their stiff Sunday collars and boots, as were their wrinkled old husbands.

Once out of St Brieuc the country was amazing. We climbed up a sheer mountain by means of zig-zags, crossing gullies and ravines by rickety viaducts. The farms looked green and prosperous — meadows down below and plough higher up. At the hill-tops were heather, yellow grass, and rocks and wherever houses could be perched, perched they were. They craned over the summits, nestled in the valleys and clung to ledges like swallows' nests. Little roads wound serpent-wise, while below us a main road had minute beetle-cars speeding along it. Having climbed to the top of the mountain our train uttered a shriek and rattled down the other side, giving us a glimpse of blue sea.

After what seemed hours, we jolted into a town of the usual tall grey houses, a church tower over all, and onto a broad quay. It was Binic at last.

We climbed down, very stiff from the wooden seats, into the arms of a dear little man who introduced himself as 'Monsieur'. He shouldered some of our cases and summoned a brawny female with a wheelbarrow for the rest and we set off down the quay, the sea on one side and tall blue-shuttered houses on the other.

People stood about in groups and women in their quaint white caps shuffled along, one and all of course talking French. We climbed a hill by means of a steep narrow lane and came out on a table land of stubble. Dusty tracks led to solitary tall houses amid pine trees. At one of these, with an unusually large garden, Monsieur stopped and proudly announced "Les Fauvettes".

The house was pleasant inside, the large rooms having bare scrubbed floors and big wide open windows. I was too tired to notice much except the big double bed in the attic I was to share with Margaret.

Never had food tasted so divine as our *dîner*! We had six courses, each more delicious than the last, and a pudding of pink whipped cream and white of egg that would have made an archangel's mouth water.

It was almost dark by the time we had coffee in the garden. And then to bed. To my relief, Margaret chose the small bed in the corner, and I went instantly to sleep.

Alas, I woke in the night feeling horribly upset and had to grope my way to the lavatory — I thanked heaven for one indoors! — which I found on a half-landing on the stairs — and several more journeys were made before I got off to sleep again.

August 30th. I awoke much refreshed and very hungry, so was disgusted at the meagre French breakfast. Aunt Lucy said that my pangs in the night were to be expected and were due to everything being cooked in olive oil; she reproached herself for not having given me a dose of the universal panacea, Dr Collis Brown's Chloradyne, without which she never sets foot aboard.

Our first act was to post cards and enquire for mail. Elizabeth and I found the post office on a quay and were rewarded by a card from Uncle Arthur, congratulating us on our arrival. I was able to take in what Binic was like. It has a large square harbour, divided by a stone pier with a lighthouse, bounded by three quays with tall houses and shops. At the western angle is the Place de L'Eglise, with its tall tower; and from here, narrow little streets branch off. Inland rise bare hills with houses craning down.

Binic Harbour

Of course, we ran down to the sea as soon as we could. A little path across a stubble field led through pine trees and then wound down the cliff. When we caught sight of the sea, we gasped with astonishment — it was beautiful beyond our dreams. The tide was in, filling a rocky cove with translucent emerald, shot with blue and purple. A margin of golden sand gave way to jagged rocks below the cliffs, which were clothed with bleached grass and pine trees, all this reflected in the clean water. But the chief charm to us was that it was completely deserted. A postcard in the town of 'La Plage' had led us to expect another Weymouth; we realised that this must have been a beach nearer the quay.

Our first act was to post cards and enquire for mail. Elizabeth and I found the post office on a quay and were rewarded by a card from Uncle Arthur, congratulating us on our arrival. I was able to take in what Binic was like. It has a large square harbour, divided by a stone pier with a lighthouse, bounded by three quays with tall houses and shops. At the western angle is the Place de L'Eglise, with its tall tower; and from here, narrow little streets branch off. Inland rise bare hills with houses craning down.

Of course, we ran down to the sea as soon as we could. A little path across a stubble field led through pine trees and then wound down the cliff. When we caught sight of the sea, we gasped with astonishment — it was beautiful beyond our dreams. The tide was in, filling a rocky cove with translucent emerald, shot with blue and purple. A margin of golden sand gave way to jagged rocks below the cliffs, which were clothed with bleached grass and pine trees, all this reflected in the clean water. But the chief charm to us was that it was completely deserted. A postcard in the town of 'La Plage' had led us to expect another Weymouth; we realised that this must have been a beach nearer the quay.

We rushed into the sea with shouts of joy; it was so clear that we could see our feet, blue green, on the honey-coloured sand when we were up to our necks.

A French family came along to bathe later on, so evidently we cannot expect to have the cove to ourselves all the time. We spent the rest of the morning scrambling over the rocks till we rounded the point and saw a whole series of beaches, just like ours only even more lovely.

At noon we returned to *dejëuner*, oh so good! Six courses again, cooked to perfection. We all felt unutterable weariness stealing over us limb by limb, and I could hardly keep my eyes open by the end of the meal. It was like being a guest at an Enchantress's feast. We all went upstairs and I slept like a log.

After delicious cups of tea, served in the garden, we went again to the beach where another surprise awaited us. The tide had gone out and a vast expanse of sand joined all the coves. No need now to climb rocks to reach them! Beautiful shells lay strewn on the sand and in rock pools were anemones, wonderful sea weeds, and tiny fish. Time flew by as we hunted among all these treasures and we were amazed when Aunt Lucy called us into *dîner*. But I was eagerly looking forward to it. I can see I shall become quite a gourmet by the time we leave Binic.

August 31st. We were rewarded for our walk to the Post Office this morning by a fat letter from AVS, containing all the latest Stogumber news. Elizabeth told me a great deal about the nice school she goes to at Oxted where two of the Churchill girls are in her form. She says that Winston is not popular in the neighbourhood; he lives at Chartwell, quite near them at Westerham. But she likes Sarah, the red-headed daughter, very much and says she has a lot of character. In return, of course, my cousin has to listen to my sagas of Bicknoller and the ponies.

We tried to sketch our cove this morning, a pearly-grey one. Not a ripple disturbed the sea, which melted into the sky; apart from green reflections under the rocks there was hardly any colour. It was difficult to paint, as its charm depended on the soft tones and the complete calm.

In the evening we went a cliff walk by a narrow path fringed with long grasses and blackberries loaded with fruit. Aunt Lucy said that no one will pick them as it is believed that the crown of thorns was woven of brambles and that the berries are cursed.

September 1st. Our bathe was not quite so nice this morning as the tide was out and we had to walk a long way before we could swim. Moreover, it was a dull grey day and although the water was warm, we grew quite chilly out of it.

In the afternoon we went down to the town and watched white-capped women washing clothes in a sunken tank at the bottom of a meadow. Then we sat on the quay at the side of *la plage*. The sea was now deep blue and an orange-sailed boat was tacking to and fro. The green cliffs had violet shadows and the rocks were flushed with rose as the sun sank. We amused ourselves by guessing which of the many people on the beach might be English and were delighted to hear a couple near us speaking our tongue. I like being abroad, for I have never known before how much I love England!

September 2nd. It was market day, so we went down and found it in process along a very narrow street, which was evil-smelling. There were countless stalls of clothes, haberdashery, bales of cloth, cheap jewellery, and boots and shoes. Others had fish and great baskets of mussels, while fruit and vegetables lay about in the wildest confusion. Crowds surged by, old wrinkled peasants and some smart townspeople, one and all bent on securing a bargain at the tops of their voices. One end of the street was reserved for produce and here were rows of women in wonderful lace caps, with baskets containing live rabbits and poultry, and there were great tubs of golden butter.

Poor Margaret felt poorly after lunch and spent the rest of the day upstairs. She is a pleasant room-mate except for a habit of snoring. However, she stops when I shout. I help her brush her hair, about which she is very particular, and she talks a good deal. She has a good memory for she tells me of things in her childhood and is fluent about her dislikes.

September 3rd.   Today we went by char-a-banc to the Isle de Brehat, leaving at eight o'clock. We were driven first to Étaples where we changed coaches. Unfortunately, it was misty so we could not see the distant views, but enjoyed one stretch where our road curved down a heathery hill to a lake in which the hill and the pine trees were reflected. A little further on we stopped to look at the ruins of an abbey. It stood at the edge of a bay dotted with islands and the sails of many fishing boats.

Our next stop was at Paimpol, quite an important fishing village. We were allowed an hour here and walked along broad quays and narrow streets where we did some shopping. It was a very picturesque village and just outside was a common bordered with lime trees where women were washing linen in a tank. We drove right round the bay of Paimpol to stop at a rocky knoll which we were encouraged to climb to see the view. It must be magnificent on a clear day; as it was, the sea and the rocky islets were shrouded in mist.

The next stop was in a hideous village where the only object of interest was a cemetery crammed with black tombstones.

Not long after this we were again on the coast and at length disembarked on a quay. We were on a long estuary, dotted with rocks, and just across the water lay the island. We were ferried over in a tiny boat and found a place among the rocks for our lunch. The mist was clearing now; before long the sun blazed from a brilliantly blue sky.

Our excellent chef at Les Fauvettes had packed us a delicious lunch and after enjoying it we found our way to the village. At least, to the hotel where our late companions on the char-a-banc were still guzzling, for the whole of Brehat is one straggling village.

We explored the island by means of little stony paths past old cottages, their gardens full of flowers, and over open spaces of tiny turf with immense slabs of granite, some of them on end like Stonehenge. Houses were dotted about like mushrooms, no roads leading to them but just footpaths. The women wore large black sunbonnets, tucked all over, that looked hot and stuffy; several were tending cows in the open spaces.

One pretty girl made a great impression on me; she was drawing water from a well, her cow meanwhile watching her with its liquid dark eyes. The handsome girl leaning over the stone parapet of the well with the sleek red cow beside her made an unforgettable picture.

At last we found what appeared to be a road, which led us to a circular hollow surrounded by old trees and quaint cottages. At the further summit we lay down in the shadow of a rock. The sun blazed down and the air was full of the hum of insects, but we were cool under our rock and fanned by a soft breeze. I dropped off in a delicious sleep, and then sat up to see an intensely blue sea and the yellow rocks blazing in the sun. The colours on Brehat are so intense that they *burn*. A little further on we found the island nearly divided by two arms of sea, only separated by a narrow ridge, with dark water and rugged rocks.

We then retraced our steps to the *place* where tea was served to us under a trellis of vines and passion flowers. They gave us little packets of biscuits, a Breton speciality, and very good. I thought the loveliest part of the island was perhaps when we stood on a high cliff. Below was a rock-encircled bay and as far as the horizon were rocks and lighthouses. Against the blue water blazed a garden of begonias, nasturtiums, fuchsia, and asters. Another colourful place was an old turretted house on a rock knoll out to sea, the turret tops and windows painted red. This combined with green turf and yellow rocks with the blue blue sea lipping against it, was brilliant enough, but as we watched, a boat came trembling out like a marvellous butterfly with orange-red sails and poised herself in the bay. The water was clear, with green and purple streaks and now the reflections of the sails rippled in it.

Poor Margaret does not like heights and particularly descending them and utterly refused to climb down from the last vantage point. It was nearly time to return to the char-a-banc; Aunt Lucy tried every persuasion and even ordered her to at least make an attempt. Elizabeth and I did our best but nothing could persuade the poor girl, tired as she was by now and thoroughly frightened. I admired Aunt Lucy immensely; she remained calm and gentle though now every moment was precious.

At last she succeeded in leading Margaret a step, Elizabeth and I took her other hand and then I supported her from behind; inch by inch we got her off the promentory and once on the path all was well.

We enjoyed the drive back, with views now visible, except for a tragic occurance at the end. Elizabeth and I longed for some chocolate and at Étaples where we again changed our char-a-banc, Elizabeth ran to a shop. Meanwhile, we got into the other coach and it was not until we were nearly out of the town that Elizabeth anxiously clutched me. "Where's my rucksack?" Her beloved sack with the camera, for which she had saved so long, and all our purchases, had been left in the other char-a-banc.

I took the entire blame but Aunt Lucy reproached us both for the rest of the way. Elizabeth pointed out that however valuable her advice might have been before the event, it was now useless, not to say trying. The driver said that he would be at Étaples early the next morning and would fetch the rucksack but, in spite of this hope, gloom was cast over the evening.

September 4th. Well before *petit déjeuner*, Elizabeth hurried to the town for her rucksack. We anxiously hung out of the window and at last I espied her returning but, alas, her hands were empty. ''Wait a moment,'' I cried to Aunt Lucy, ''she may have it over her back,'' and, sure enough, she had. I ran to meet her and we returned singing 'See the conquering hero comes' until heads popped out from the windows to see what *les folles Anglaises* were up to.

We felt quite mad in the evening and danced in and out of the black shadows of our pine trees for over an hour, composing ballets and performing feats unknown to any dancing instructor.

September 5th. I am getting anxious about the School Certificate and last night dreamt that a horrible fat woman whom I was sure knew nothing, was marking my papers. I had to sit by to watch her writing 'failed' all over my best subjects.

AVS is a brick; she sends *The Times* every day and writes twice a week. Uncle Arthur writes too; with his spidery hand he gets more on a card than most people on a letter. The party at Hardown breaks up tomorrow.

As we went down the cliff to bathe this morning, we heard a sound as if kittens were mewing. We thought it must be young seagulls but after a search I found a tiny white fluffy kitten, its blue eyes open, at the edge of a large rubbish-tip. Scrambling up, I found, to my horror, six more. I thought someone must have thrown them away but Aunt Lucy said perhaps their mother had brought them there.

Margaret writing home

However, they were still crying piteously on our return and I could not bear it; I had to stop my ears. We felt the only thing to do was to ask kind Monsieur to inspect them and if he thought them orphans to drown them. This he did, and my heart has bled ever since. I cannot understand the mentality of someone who could throw such enchanting little creatures away alive and leave them to starve. If only I could get hold of the wretch — but my French would not be

45

equal to my feelings!

We went a country walk after tea, following the little river that runs into the harbour. It led us through meadows with high woods on one side, the railway viaduct on the other. We soon came to a mill with a huge water-wheel; it was also a farm, and a dear little puppy came bouncing out to lick our hands.

We walked along the mill-leat, which the miller had sensibly planted with fruit trees; they and willows made a 'tunnel of green gloom'. Suddenly, there was a flutter and two blue flames flashed down the green tunnel — kingfishers. I had never seen them before and was entranced.

September 7th. We searched for cowrie shells in the morning and in the afternoon set out for a long walk, taking biscuits for tea. We went past old grey farms and took field paths and shady lanes like those in Devon. There was indeed nothing foreign except the landscape seen from a height, when the tall trees, their branches lopped, and the great numbers of poplars and aspens in the valleys, with the yellow hill-tops shining in the heat, did make one feel oneself abroad.

We thought we would call at a farm for milk to drink with our biscuits, but it proved easier said than done. At our first stop, a brown-eyed man at the door of a cow-shed absorbed in watching the cows munching within, said that Madame was out and that he was afraid of giving us milk from the wrong pan. So we refreshed ourselves with the luscious blackberries in the hedges and went on.

At the next farm, everyone was out; we had passed the women burning weeds in the fields. All over the country people were busy at this; it reminded me of a scene in *Travels with a Donkey*. The bitter blue smoke drifting above the dry landscape was just as Stevenson describes.

At length we arrived at a large farm where a man and a girl were loading a cart with straw. We put our request and the girl replied that we might go in and ask Madame if we wished. So we trooped in through a cobbled yard with a big tree in the centre and knocked at an open door. A voice called *"Entrez"*, and we plunged into gloom.

We found ourselves in a large kitchen where a handsome woman sat in the window. She expressed no surprise at our entry and said that the cows had not yet been milked and, of course, we did not wish for cold? It was quite fresh, she added; it had been milked at noon, but, of course, we wanted it hot from the cow?

On being reassured, she gave us chairs round the table and poured out bowls of milk. It was a very large, dim, kitchen with hardly any furniture; a smart new dresser, the chairs, table, and a sewing-machine were almost all. But evidently, farms are allied

46

the world over, for the usual china dogs and cats gazed mournfully from the dresser, with 'Presents from Binic' and photographs on the mantlepiece. The fireplace was immense, running the whole length of the room.

Madame talked very politely, telling us that they kept eighteen cows and had a car. Her two little girls, very pretty with long curly hair, came running in, and on being given a biscuit each, went into fits of giggles and were chased from the room by their mother. As we left we caught sight of a lovely 'back 'us' with old oak beams, copper pots and pans, and flitches of bacon.

September 8th. After a bathe, Elizabeth came with me for our letters. There were several and I saw that one was from Miss Benison. I felt dazed and sick; it seemed an age before the girl had stamped it and passed it through the *guichet*. With trembling hands I tore it open: it said 'Congratulations upon your pass'. The words swam, and I know now that the heroine's feelings as she opens the all-important letter in a novel are by no means exaggerated.

Further down, Miss Benison continued '3rd class honours are more than I dared hope for, but you deserve them as you worked so hard.' Actually, honours! Beyond my dreams, even 3rd class ones. We walked back with my mind in a whirl and I spent the morning on the beach, writing the news to relatives and friends.

September 9th. It was a scorching day and after our swim — I can swim much better now — Elizabeth and I found a secluded nook in the rocks and lay naked until we roasted through and through.

If it was hot in the morning, it was almost unbearable after *déjeuner*; we changed into our coolest frocks and sat under the pine trees in the garden. After tea, as the tide was out, we walked across the bay by the town; it was pleasant on the firm sand. The tide came racing in so fast that we only just reached the little bay on which we had set our hearts.

It was worth a visit; the narrow valley running down to it had a sparkling brook between beds of flags and the steep sides were of bracken and heather with bare granite rocks. We followed up the brook and presently came to tall oaks and ash trees, the stream accompanying us so closely that sometimes its cresses and mint strayed onto the path.

Wood pigeons were cooing and I liked the place so much that I stayed behind to have it all to myself. We walked back along the cliffs in and out of gorse and heather, all the while looking down to the translucent green sea sucking and gurgling on rocks below.

September 10th. Elizabeth and I sketched the town from the lighthouse this morning, Margaret sitting with us. Boats were coming in with a rustle and swish of their great russet sails and settling down in the harbour. On the steps of the lighthouse sat an old fisherman, motionless, staring out to sea. He had a crutch and was evidently a cripple who came every day to look at the sea he had toiled on so long. He had a beautiful face with wonderful eyes.

Back at the Les Fauvettes, I found three letters, one from Rex with some stamps I have long wanted. He must have remembered from looking at my album at Manor Farm and got them especially. There was a budget of news from AVS and a letter from Mother. The bathroom at West Hill has been tiled and a washbasin installed and, better still, a lavatory-pan! So the horrible slop-pails will no longer have to be carried down, past the front door to the WC at the end of the hall.

September 11th. The night was so hot that I could not sleep, and restless and sticky, resolved that I would bathe as soon as I woke. Accordingly, I hurried down, unbolted the door and ran out to a fragrant world of pale sunshine and dew. The sea was calm and smooth as oil, melting into the sky with no horizon. Just above, the sun threw a broad glittering pathway; and not a soul about. I had a perfect bathe, and how good rolls and coffee tasted after it!

I have letters by every post; today one from Summer Tolley and a priceless one from Miss Hammett, full of advice about sketching; she evidently thinks I do nothing else.

September 12th. After a great deal of swimming — I now go fearlessly out of my depth — I found a letter from Narney, saying that she is due for leave on the 20th and could I be at West Hill, as it would be so boring otherwise. I also had the *West Somerset Gazette* and the usual advertisement announced that next term begins on September 27th. So I could go to London and still have a few days left for riding. It was a thrilling *Gazette* this week, full of Dunster Show, at which both Kim and Duncan won prizes, and an account of a fête at Manor House, Crowcombe, where 'Miss Winifred Foster gave a delightful display of classical dancing'.

September 13th. I was the only bather today, which was cool and grey and inclined to drizzle. We lay on the beach telling stories and breaking off for the next to continue. Our hero began as an impoverished knife-grinder; Aunt Lucy introduced a fairy who whirled him off to the Sahara to find his heart's desire. Elizabeth and Margaret callously left him there suffering tortures of thirst in

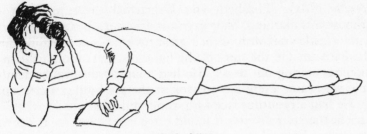

Elizabeth lisant

vast tracts of sand, but I brought him to an encampment of cannibals where at least he had water. He escaped the cooking-pot by giving the Chieftain his beautiful red beard and, finally, Aunt Lucy brought him on a magic carpet to an ivory palace.

The Princess therein was expecting a knife-grinder as her husband so expressed no surprise, merely remarking "At last thou hast come, my beloved." Elizabeth married them and they dined on roast peacocks with their tails on.

In the evening we went by train to St Honoré and after taking a charming lane pushed our way down a steep wooded combe to the beach. The sea was roaring across flat sands and a group of fishermen with their wives and children were stretching nets to catch prawns on the tide. We found wonderful shells there; large flat cockles, red-brown oysters, and dish-shaped ones with blue and purple streaks.

On our walk home we came to a straggling hamlet with a nice farm where a woman and her daughter were straining milk. "Oh yes, certainly you shall have some," and she hastily began to braid her hair, which was in two long plaits. She took us to a room in which were two huge beds, at least four feet above the floor. There were two immense walnut presses and the table at which we were invited to sit.

The very handsome and garrulous farmer's wife brought us wine glasses and opened one of the presses. It was full from top to bottom with linen neatly piled; she took a cloth to polish our glasses and brought a large soup-tureen of milk, warm from the cow. Her pretty daughter kept creeping in to have a look at us but was severely scolded and shut out.

Then we were taken to see six sleek cows lying contentedly in the deep straw of their shed, and a huge glossy cart horse. The woman was a friendly soul and came out to show us the way, shouting directions and blessings long after we had turned the corner.

As we came down the lovely combe that we explored on the 9th a large hawk was sitting in the path, unlike any I know. The tide was out so we walked home across the sands.

September 14th. We began our walk early this afternoon, buying some heavenly cakes at a little bakers in the market street. For some time we kept to the dusty road in the valley of the river Ilk; Rue des Moulins as it is appropriately named, for there are several mills clacking away along the stream. A little green lane then led us through water meadows to another road, where we tossed up at every cross. Our walk thus depending upon caprice gave a most exhilarating and carefree feeling.

The houses here all being up on the plateau, we did not see one in the valley save the mills. The white road led between poplars and aspens that kept up a perpetual whisper, like the rustle of silk. But when we had climbed a steep lane, we came out on the rolling land of stubble, dotted with farms. Everywhere people were working in the fields, blue smoke drifting from their fires.

By and by we came to a little village of grey stone cottages and farms set round cross roads. One farm, called Nerrepot, was especially picturesque, a great walnut tree shading its gables. Under this a rosy old lady was drawing water from the well; she told us to go to another entrance, so we made our way through the farmyard, where pigeons were strutting, and found the front door opening on the pig-styes.

Within, the quaint farm was perfect, with old oak and walnut presses inlaid with shining brass. In each corner stood enormous beds, elaborately carved. One was an old Breton closed one like a box of black carved wood. A small hole in the centre revealed snowy sheets, but even this was partially veiled with lace curtains. Over the mantle were photographs and ivory crucifixes, and a highly-polished oak stairway led up at one end of the room, closed halfway by a massive panelled door. Below it, more steps led down, presumably to back regions; an open door revealed a smaller kitchen, where an open hearth held a blazing fire under the largest cauldron I have ever seen.

A bowl of milk was brought to us in the window, with cups of thick earthenware, gaily coloured and glazed. I admired them greatly, and was told that they were cider cups. The woman seemed shy, and her old husband was obviously terrified of us.

Elizabeth and I sketched the farm while Aunt Lucy and Margaret strolled up and down. Heads popped out of all the gateways and children appeared to look as if by magic; even cows and a horse came up to have a look. It was not long before we heard excited voices and beheld Aunt Lucy and Margaret besieged by two old women, a girl, several infants, an assortment of hens, two dogs and a cow. We saw wild gesticulations on every side, while a perfect torrent of French proceeded from the women.

Though Aunt Lucy has lived so long in France, she understands little and her vocabulary is limited to a few phrases, so we guessed she must be in a difficult position. But the group looked so funny that we were in fits of laughter. They were being asked about "the big England", Are there any poor?" "Is the butter dear?" "Do people keep hens and how much are eggs a dozen?" "Is it true that in England everyone is rich?" and were proudly told that Madame had been twice to Jersey.

Before long Madame herself came clattering along in her sabots, attended by a small grandson and another cow. She was a nice old lady with piercing black eyes, innumerable wrinkles, and a deep masculine voice.

Aunt Lucy and Margaret left us to finish our sketch, but we walked quickly back, singing and soon overtook them. The worst of these walks is that Aunt Lucy crawls, which I find very tiring.

September 16th. We went to the market again today, hoping to see some of the various dames in whose kitchens we have been imbibing milk. But it was impossible in such a crowd, where every other woman has a wrinkled face, a black stiff dress and a lace cap. We did some marketing, buying gifts to take home, and then had a bathe and a scramble over the rocks.

When we got in from our walk in the evening, Madame — Monsieur's sister-in-law, who does the cooking and is a perfect darling, wrinkles, lace cap and all — told us that they all were going to an entertainment given by *Les Jeunes Gens De Binic*, under the patronage of St Julien. We decided to go ourselves: Aunt Lucy said that as there are no W I or G F S in France, the social events are given by the girls and boys separately; no one would dream of their acting or singing together. At St Omar they had them every term, lasting for hours on end.

We went down to the quay to find a large crowd outside the hall, and got seats rather at the back, hemmed in by gesticulating families. We were packed like sardines and it was fearfully hot in spite of open windows. And the noise! Everyone shouted with all the force of his or her lungs and there was a strong smell of sweet scent and hair-oil.

An enormous curé about eight feet tall came in and sat on a packing case in the gangway next to me. At least, he was partly on the case and partly on me. He was a perfect dear and produced handfuls of bon-bons from his cassock which he shared with us all.

At last, after a frantic ringing of handbells, and appeals from a burly priest, silence fell, and a tinny piano struck up. The curtains parted to reveal five or six very nervous little boys, who sang a long song. The audience kindly joined in and by the time we reached the tenth verse we were all shouting once more at the tops of our voices.

Two fierce ladies wearing pince-nez turned round and said "Sh" so sharply that I nearly died of fright.

When the noise had died down the curtain rose once more on a screaming farce entitled 'A Qui est le Neveu?' The seven characters were each more nervous than the last, but warmed to their task. I must say that I think a French audience far easier than an English one, for everyone roared at the slightest joke from the start, whereas we don't thaw until halfway through.

Between the acts we had songs, some comic and some sentimental, all very well received.

The evening ended with another farce, 'Les Deux Sourds,' amid howls of laughter. In this there was actually a boy dressed as a girl; very charming with the closest of shingles, red lips and an apple-green frock with gold spangles. True, her arms were brawny and her voice gruff but she really was a beauty.

We walked home with Madame, Yvonne and Jeanette, all of us full of the wonders we had beheld.

September 18th. After such a hot day yesterday when we had to get into the sea all day long to cool off, we took an excursion and set out by train to Plouard. The stuffy journey took a whole hour and by then it was even hotter.

We crawled out of the dust and glare to an inn, where we sat in a cave of black shadows and drank citron and soda. Fortunately, we found a green meadow and ate our lunch in the shade of some elms and then set out to the beach, three kilometres away.

The road wound down a beautiful valley; a stream broadened into a lake covered with water-lillies, and there were fine old trees. At last we saw the sea and came out in a little village. One or two inns had striped awnings and blue and red shutters that looked gay, and a grove of lime trees shaded the place. The stream ran out between grandly sweeping cliffs.

Elizabeth and I lost no time before bathing and then basked in the sun on hot pebbles until it was time for tea at one of the inns. We walked back leisurely, enjoying a shady lane high on one side of the valley. Already the leaves were turning from sombre green to golden brown, and today I heard robins singing, a sure sign that autumn is near.

It seemed a long walk, five miles at least, though Aunt Lucy pointed out that a kilometre is less than a mile and that it was only three of them!

Our train was very late and by the time it came in the sun was setting grandly in a sea of orange fire.

Dusk fell quickly, lights twinkled out, and a large golden moon

p.8, etc. At Manor Farm. Standing: Molly Tapper, Anne
Sitting: Pamela English, Rex Sangar, A V S, Winifred Foster

p.5, etc. Captain Evans Smith at Stogumber

p.21, etc. Mother

p.20, Miss Mary Rossetti

p.53, Christopher Nickalls,
one of 'my two small nephews'

p.26, etc. 'I know
that I shall like Elizabeth'

p.12, etc. Winifred Foster dancing

Chaps.1 & 2 Molly Tapper

Chaps.1 & 2 Pamela English,
Mrs Hunt's grand-daughter

p.80. Constance Michell

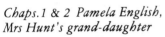

The West Somerset Foxhounds at St Audries

p.17. The farm and a meet at Cloutsham

Chap.3. Anne and Helen

Chap.3. Mother and Father at Hardown

p.61, etc. At Weacombe:
A V S

The sitting-room

14

The cottage

Anne

16

The future: Bushey Art School
Frank Lee Michell

climbed up in the east.

I was dog-tired, and dozed uncomfortably with the jolting of the train shaking my bones and the confused babel of all the Breton passengers. However, the walk up from the station was lovely, the moon whitening Binic and gleaming on the sea.

September 20th. We spent our last day yesterday lazily, in preparation for the journey, bathing and basking, and sad to leave our lovely cove.

After bidding melancholy farewells to everyone at les Fauvettes, we left about 9.30 a.m. It has been a wonderful holiday.

CHAPTER V

September 21st — October 23rd, 1926

❋✾✳ ❋✾✳

SEPTEMBER 21st. We had a moonlight crossing and two comfortable cabins, but Elizabeth preferred to stay on deck and I could not sleep for the slap of the waves. So I was tired by the time we had spent an hour with the customs, boarded the train, and I had finally arrived at Highgate on a No. 7 tram.

My suitcase was terribly heavy to carry up West Hill and I was greeted by Mother and Rayne but no Narney. To quote her own words "that blighted matron" had cancelled her leave.

I was exhausted, and when Rayne said that she was leaving after lunch and Mother that she had an invitation to a luncheon party and was sorry that I should be alone in the afternoon, I burst into tears. I sobbed loudly, without caring how much noise I made, and declared that this was the limit! I had come all that way to see them; it just showed that they cared not a pin for me, and I heartily wished I had gone straight back to Somerset.

Mother appeared much surprised but said that she would wire her friends to put off her luncheon, whereat I dried my eyes and replied "I should jolly well hope so". However, there were several letters to read; one from Mrs Evans Smith, one from AVS, and one from Joy Parkinson enclosing snap-shots taken at the Seatown bathing picnic. These cheered me up and I admired the new bathroom and fresh wallpaper on stairs and landings and began to feel home not such a bad place after all, especially when I sniffed the aroma of dust, books, and leather in the study.

Presently in came my two small nephews, attended by a nice Swiss girl. They were sweet; Christer just the same only able to talk now in a shy little voice. Robert is a tiny thin little creature with deep-set brown eyes. I watched them eat their dinner and then saw them all off in a taxi; they were going to Brighton to stay with the Blacks.

Christer

54

Father and Dicky wanted to hear all about Brittany when they came in. We spent a cosy evening in the study, blue tobacco smoke wreathing up. A typical Garnett evening — but it will be lovely to be back in Somerset tomorrow!

September 22nd. I arrived at Taunton as expected at 2.30, although Mother had found me a train that meant changing at Bristol, and AVS met me wreathed in smiles.

She had some shopping to do so we we walked into the town and she asked "Would you like your Christmas present now?" Of course I said yes, and she took me into a shop where they had a splendid second-hand bicycle. It was only a year old and in good condition. Now I shall be able to get to Bicknoller in record time, and to the station.

I did not stop talking once I think, through the journey home and our tea — there was so much to tell about Hardown and Brittany. Winifred had tea all ready and afterwards we went into the lane where she and AVS tried to teach me to ride the bike — far more difficult than a horse.

and Robert

It was a perfect evening, blue and still with frost in the air. The sun set in a glory of wine-colour paling to a dull rose; blue smoke from the cottage chimneys rose straight against the green hills. It is lovely to be back in England — the trees are their proper shapes again.

September 23rd. Winifred came with me to Bicknoller, holding me on the new cycle — I ride quite well on the flat but am terrified of mounting. We found Captain Evans Smith just setting off in the Delage and his poor wife in bed with neuralgia; however, she was extremely pleased to see us.

Then down to the stables where I had to submit to a stream of personal remarks from Mr Frost: "You're much fatter; I like the way the Frenchies have cut your hair". He said that Bicknoller had been wildly excited as Mrs Jennings at the Post Office said she had seen the result of the exam in a paper long before Miss Benison or AVS had heard. The rumours went flying round the village, no one knowing whether to believe it or not. Filbert threw Duddles the other day. I was delighted to hear that, as now we are quits. We rode to Weacombe as he said there was a cottage to let — his mother thinks of settling there so they are looking for a home. I pricked up my ears at this and was all agog as we trotted up the lane. The empty cottage is the last of the few that face the stream behind Weacombe House, and so is just at the mouth of the coombe. A prettier place could not be imagined — behind rise the larches of the plantation, opposite, the hill-path to Bicknoller makes an opening in the woods and the stream runs down from the coombe between cressy banks. Through the trees at Weacombe House is a fine view of the wide valley, the Brendons beyond.

Three of the cottages are modern, two semi-detached, the empty one a little apart, built of brick covered with Virginia creeper, a tiled roof and a nice garden behind sloping up the hill. In front there is a small grass patch with rose beds, opposite a most picturesque thatched dwelling, rather hovel than cottage.

Old cottage at Weacombe

Mr Frost dismounted and peered into the windows. "H'm, yes its too small for us," he said. "Couldn't get our furniture in there." He reported a good kitchen with scullery behind, fair sized parlour, and three bedrooms.

I drank it all in, and asked what the rent might be. "Oh, about £25 a year, I expect." I resolved to tell AVS about it.

We rode along the hill path to Bicknoller. Mr Frost killed a wounded pigeon on the way and gave it to me. Then along the further path to Quantock Moor where Filbert became very naughty and excited Jane; altogether we had a lively ride up and down the steep slopes of the path.

It was wonderful to be back. I felt I could kiss every tree that we passed. There is nothing to equal the Quantocks, especially now when they are changing from green to russet gold.

Winifred and I sat with the poor neuralgia sufferer for some time; she asked us to come tomorrow when there is to be a practice polo on the field at Kilve.

September 24th. AVS was poorly today; too much excitement at my return, we think. She was interested to hear of the Weacombe cottage but is not hopeful and says we must find out more about it. She stayed in bed and I ran up to Dr Rogers and asked him to call. He said she had a touch of bronchitis and should be well in a day or two.

So we packed up sandwiches for our tea and I cycled off to

Bicknoller, only getting off twice all the way, and once was involuntarily. I came round a corner and rode slap into Winifred, who had stopped for a flock of sheep.

I rode to Kilve and it was announced that Winifred should ride back. We went up the combe and straight over the hill. A path bordered by huge beech trees led us gently down to the green at Holford, which has several old cottages edging it. Here there was a beautiful view up the wooded glen to the purple moors above and the wide valley stretching to Bridgwater Bay. The Captain was very genial and asked endless questions about Brittany, telling me in turn of his experiences in France. All he remembers of St Omar, where the Cowlishaws have been living, is that he ate twenty-four cakes at one go when in hospital there.

I had not been to the new polo club at Kilve before, though I had heard about it and was most interested. It is just a field but there were several cars lined up when we arrived; the Storeys, some Kilve people, and the Archers. Mr Frost gave me a stick and a ball and told me to knock the ball about. I found it extremely difficult and it made my wrist ache.

We saw quite a good game; Duddles played very well indeed. His mother is proud, as he has won a cup by getting into the finals at the Dunster Tournament. It *is* good as he has not played at all till this season. I sat with Mrs Frost, listening to her endless flow. It is not surprising that her son will not allow her to speak during play.

We ate a colossal tea as both Mrs Evans Smith and Mrs Frost had brought extra food for us, not to mention our own. Going back in the car, I learnt that the Weacombe cottage belongs to Mr Sadler, Guy's uncle, at Weacombe House.

While waiting for Winifred to arrive I was asked to help catch some ponies in a field opposite the inn, and, of course, was only too pleased. Duddles also enlisted the aid of Stephen Vernon, who happened to be about, saying "We really need four; they're devils to catch". They certainly were, the brown mare being the worst. She laid back her ears and was off like the wind whenever we came near her. The other two, Gipsy and Marcus, galloped off too out of sheer devilment.

The brown mare seemed bewitched. Time and time again we drove her into a corner, time and time again she broke through. It was rather alarming as she often made straight for one, her ears laid back and her teeth barred in a wicked grin. The field, moreover, was large with tangled grass and rushes so that we tripped and fell as we ran.

At long last we did catch her, closing up, very gently, to where she stood panting and wild-eyed. The brute! We could have killed her, but had to be loving, slipping on the head-stall with soothing pats and caresses, all the while cursing her under our breath. It had taken us a good half-hour. Duddles said that the other night they were at it for over an hour and the Captain was weeping with rage at the end.

September 25th. We went to Taunton today for shopping, before Winifred went back to school. I saw her off at the station, where she got into a carriage with our new school-mistress. For Miss Webster has left to be married. Winifred is desolate and I shall miss her too. But I have heard so much of her recently that the very name makes me want to scream.

AVS wrote to Mr Sadler yesterday, applying for the cottage. I wonder what the answer will be?

I was not to wonder for long, for this evening in walked Guy. AVS was so overcome with excitement that she had to run upstairs and I entertained him until her return. He said that he had come about the cottage and that it was to be let at £25 a year. AVS said that she could manage that, and were many people after it? Guy said he thought not and that she need not feel she was turning down any working people. Would we go over on Monday? His uncle would be about with the keys and would be delighted to show us over it.

Wild excitement!

September 27th. I was really supposed to start school today but AVS could not bear to deprive me of the pleasure of going to Weacombe and let me off. We drove over in Sully's Maxwell — a gloriously sunny day with the wind chasing cloud shadows. Mr Sadler escorted us through his grounds and up the lane. He is a dear old gentleman; pink cheeks, blue eyes, and white hair. When he laughs he throws his head right back and does it most heartily.

The cottage was very nice inside, the sun streaming in through casement windows; the kitchen and scullery have cheerful red-tiled floors and oh, the views from the bedrooms!

Mr Sadler seemed anxious that we should like it, and drew attention to all the good points. The worst are that there is no water laid on and only an earth-closet outside the back door. But the stream flows ten yards from the gate with a dipping-place for drinking and ordinary water so it really does not matter.

After locking up the cottage, Mr Sadler took us up the combe, to the gate at the end of the larch plantation. AVS was enraptured with it all — it certainly is something to have the great hills sweeping down to your gate. Our future landlord — as we hope — discoursed of the hundreds of foxes and the damage they do, at least £100 a year on his land alone. He took us round his garden on our return; he is a keen gardener and had beds of seedlings and cuttings and a

The larch wood

wonderful collection of rare and semi-tropical shrubs.

Before we left, he would visit his solicitor and get a deed drawn up. AVS replied that she would be only too pleased to take the cottage provided the rates were not too high, and asked him to find out what they might be.

If we were excited before our visit to the cottage what were we now that we had actually seen it? We talked of nothing else and hoped and prayed the rates would be low.

September 30th. AVS had the deed from the solicitor this morning, but no word as to the rates. So she wrote a note asking again, and if we could go to Weacombe to measure for curtains, etc. To her dismay, Mr Read on being asked, said he thought the rates might be £10, and Amby Couch thought £8.

This was worrying, as either would be out of the question. So I cycled off with the note. Mr Sadler was out so there was no relief.

I went on to Bicknoller where Mrs Evans Smith was most comforting — very much pleased at the idea of our being at Weacombe and sure the rates could not possibly be more than £5. She sent me down to the stables to ask the Captain what he thought.

He and Mr Frost were attending the chestnut mare, who was blistered yesterday. She took it very badly, plunging and rearing so that they cannot leave her for a moment although she is secured by ropes and a cradle. To my query the Captain said "Oh, lord no, Anne, the rates couldn't be more than £4."

In my relief, I had a good game with Mr Frost's puppies, with a lighter heart than I had had all day. To my surprise there was Genius, the hound, contentedly gnawing a bone. He slipped off from cub-hunting yesterday and had made for his old home.

In the evening, who should come in but kind Guy. He brought a note from his uncle saying that the rates are £1.12.1d and would we come tomorrow to measure?

October 1st. Besley drove us to Weacombe in his dog-cart; I did enjoy it, it's a long while since I had been in one. For the first time, I noticed the apples in the Vellow orchards; they are thick on the trees, some as red as blood.

We found workmen at the cottage, filling in nail-holes in the walls and other little things. We measured everything in the bright sunshine; I began to feel it home already. If only I could live in it and go to art school in Taunton. It will break my heart to leave it for London and I am afraid AVS will have rather a struggle to keep things going between her paying guests. But she has had several articles accepted lately and a request for a series from the *Westminster Gazette* and 'Sufficient unto the day . . .'.

October 2nd. We went to Taunton by the 9.45 to buy furniture for the cottage. At Chapman's second-hand shop we found an extremely nice man who knew just what was wanted and produced it from forgotten corners.

Shopping in Taunton

We chose white enamelled things for two bedrooms; the third will have to remain bare for the present; and arm chairs for the parlour. There was a pretty mahogany writing desk, fitted with drawers, marked £3.10s. The man said "H'm, a mistake but not mine," and quickly marked it sold, assuring us that once so written the mistake could not be rectified.

Turning to the kitchen, he found us a dresser, two tables, and chairs. At the shop, proper, we bought rush mats, parlour and stair carpets, and buff material for curtains. Then to lunch at Maynards, tired and happy, and on to an ironmongers for pots and pans and a china shop for the dinner service and pie-dishes, etc.

We were exhausted by the time we got to the station and more exhausted still after the walk home, but excited and happy.

Mother sent AVS sheets and towels when she first heard the news of Broad Oak and is to send more. She says it is what she regards as a happy duty for a daughter setting up house and that AVS must look at it in that light.

October 4th.   We went to Elworthy today, to give Gordon a watch that AVS has bought him in memory of her brother Walter. The weather was still and misty with a blue haze. We enjoyed the walk.

The Landers are boarding at Whites Farm till they go to Bournemouth, having removed from the old Rectory; we found Mrs Hayes getting their tea and Miss Lander toasting scones at the back 'us fire. She was friendly and Mrs Hayes obviously relieved and surprised to find that we did not fly at each other's throats. There has long been a coolness between AVS and Mrs L. ever since we dined with her and the son kissed me behind the door when his mother sent him to "bring up a bottle of booze for the ladies".

Mrs Hayes was as usual full of news. We could not tell her much as she had heard all about Weacombe from Baker Jones. Ned came in to a cosy tea; afterwards Gordon took me round and Miss Lander came out to chase him round the ricks in the moor barton.

He was pleased with his watch! We made him guess what was in the box and when he couldn't, told him to put it to his ear. When he heard it ticking he became perfectly crimson, his eyes growing larger and larger. I went with him and Ned to drive the cows to drink in Tilsey land as they are very short of water at the farm. We drove them home for milking and Mrs Hayes came with us once again up Mondsborough.

October 5th.   I cycled to Bicknoller dodging heavy storms today; it was rough with a blustering wind roaring in the trees. Inky clouds rolled up so quickly that heavy rain fell where an instant before the sky had been clear blue. But I like that sort of day. I like the rushing, tearing sound of wind, and the sudden effects of light and shade. My bike and I were tossed along the road like feathers.

I found a very busy Captain, single handed, as Winter had left till the spring and the boy and Mr Frost are on holiday. He was sorry he had nothing for me to ride as it was too stormy to risk the ponies.

Instead, I had a happy time doing odd jobs for his wife, among them going to pick blackberries in the top field. It was grand up there, the wind so strong that I could not stand against it. The country all round me was picked out in vivid colours against the rolling black clouds. Punch, Prudence, and Cheetah were having a gallop and looked splendid, their tails streaming in the wind.

I stopped for lunch and was teased by the Captain as usual; however, I got off more lightly than the luckless puppy who was seized by its tail and hauled onto its master's lap to be pulled about.

After lunch, he saddled Duncan for me; he himself was to ride Robin, who had to be fetched from a field. No sooner did I reach the drive gate than Duncan stuck and would not go on, do what I would.

"Let me get on the brute," said the Captain, so I dismounted and held the spare tack. Poor Duncan; he danced about with his head in the air for a while, but all to no purpose. He had to go on. By degrees he calmed down, I got on, and we went peaceably forward. We got very wet in a driving storm, when the rain stung like bullets, but grew warm again when the sun came out. I found AVS busily packing, on my return.

October 9th. I had an invitation to lunch at the Middletons, so cycled there today. Once I had climbed Ashpier it did not take long, though I had to wait under the great beeches on the top road for a heavy storm. It was grand to skim down Whetstone Nap.

Mrs Middleton came running out when she heard the gate bang and gave me a warm welcome. I was introduced to a nephew, a red-faced young farmer with huge horny hands. He spoke such broad Somerset that I had difficulty in understanding him, used as I am to the dialect; he had come to see his uncle on a motor-cycle. It seemed most incongruous to think of a man straight out of *Lorna Doone* with a motor engine.

Replete after a huge dinner of roast fowl and apple tart, we sat round a roaring fire and told each other all the news we could think of and then, after feeding the poultry, I took my leave and had to walk nearly all the way home as I had two punctures.

October 10th. We moved today! First of all Mr Read loaded a waggon with our luggage and set off, with a highly excited little boy beside him. Then a nice woman named Westcott arrived to go with us and sundry other parcels in Sully's car, and we said farewell to Manor Farm and kind Mrs Read.

Of course, there was nothing to do at the cottage till the waggon arrived, but at last it came creaking up the lane and we helped to unload. Then came a picnic lunch, sitting on the stairs to eat cold chicken out of brown paper.

Soon after, Chapman's van came; the men were very quick at unloading and placing the furniture. Mrs Westcott and I unpacked exciting packing cases containing the china, etc., washed the dishes, and put them away, my first task being to get out a bucket and fetch water from the brook.

It was astonishing how soon the bareness gave place to a furnished home. The men laid the carpets and even hung the curtains; by the time they left, everything was in place. We just had time to clean ourselves and have tea when Sully came with my bicycle and to fetch

Mrs Wescott. AVS and I were alone in our cottage at last.

When we sat down to supper, the range glowing and the lamplight shining on the pots and pans and crockery on the dresser, it was as if we had been there for years.

October 11th. It was thrilling to open my eyes in my blue and white bedroom with the glorious view from the window. We were down early and having breakfast in our cheerful kitchen when the postman came with an enormous parcel of linen from Mother.

Cottages at Williton

Then I cycled to Williton station for my school train, allowing forty minutes — it only took ten! It was not so quick coming home, with the long hill to climb but I enjoyed it, knowing I was coming home to the cottage. Besides, it is a beautiful road, the Quantocks ahead and the valley and Exmoor behind.

James Pigg was sitting on our doorstep, his mistress within, come to be our first caller. We took her round proudly and she admired everything.

October 14th. Punctures again; I have taken the cycle to be mended and so had to walk the three miles to the station. It was very wet but I kept dry under two pairs of stockings, my Burberry, and mackintosh hat.

Karen came to painting class with Miss Hammett; it was nice to see her again. She has been staying in London, has had her hair shingled and looked very much the 'finished article', having decided to leave school.

Afterwards, I went to see Miss Briggs, our old

headmistress; she had quite a tea-party on and we sat on small chairs and made polite conversation. There was a good fire and an abundance of delicious cakes, so I felt warm and happy till a sudden lull. Miss Briggs was asking in what subjects I had Honours and I had just said "Botany, Drawing," when there fell a deathly silence. Of course, I stopped too, but "Well, go on" said Miss Briggs. "Botany, Drawing?" "French, Geography, Scripture, and English," I rushed on, wishing myself at the bottom of the sea. Everyone looked impressed and a lady said "Splendid; of course, you intend going to University?" "No," I said feeling a worm. "I'm — I'm going to try to learn to draw horses."

October 16th. We walked to our new church at St Audries for Matins. The open park sloping to the sea with autumn coloured woods and the russet Quantocks above make a wonderful setting for the little Tractarian Church. Mr Sadler caught us up at the gate, and apologised for not having been to see us. He is a delightful old gentleman and I am sure will become a great friend, but I fear we have exchanged our parson for a worse. Mr Rust, an old man with a flowing beard, preached a most hesitant sermon. We shall miss Amby's eloquent flow.

October 19th. Capt. Brandling came out today to give me a lesson on drawing horses from the life. I overtook him just after I left the station and we cycled together to Weacombe, where he admired everything, especially a magnificent Florence oil-stove that Dicky has just sent AVS. The kitchen range is now named Dora because no coal is allowed on her after eight o'clock. As we have very little coal we only burn logs in the parlour.

Capt. Brandling and I cycled on to Bicknoller, where we leant on a gate to sketch Duncan. It was extremely cold with a bitter east wind whistling down our necks, and after a while we went to the stable and worked in a box. The Captain was about and came to crack jokes, even colder than we were. Tea at Weacombe was very cosy after this; we sat round the kitchen table and AVS and Capt. Brandling exchanged Zummerzet stories. He speaks the dialect very well.

October 23rd. A fine day at last; how blessed to see the sun again. I cleaned and black-leaded the grate before leaving for Bicknoller; luckily I enjoy housework for AVS has exceedingly high standards.

The Captain and I rode out together, he on a brown gelding and I on Filbert. We went to Vellow to have the gelding shod; on the way I was given an interesting lecture on the correct theory of balancing a horse and how the French idea is wrong — I am to be lent a book on the subject.

While the shoeing was in progress, I rode up the lane and round again. On the hill it was wonderful to see a sunny landscape hazy with filmy clouds and a rosy bloom on the plough. I like to see a field half ploughed with the grey-gold stubble cut across by rich streaming red loam, the rooks straddling over it. I like the elms now too, yellow at the tips, and the beeches glowing orange-red. The oaks are russet to match the bracken. I rather wish I had not a camera for a brain, but it is in colour, not black and white. I find myself thinking now: what paint could I use for that? It is rather a tiresome habit.

Back at the stables, I drew horses in the yard; the Evans Smiths had gone out and there was no one about. The sun streamed down, the ponies lazed with their heads drooping out of the boxes, the wind rustled straws about the yard and now and then a noisy flock of sparrows whirred past or chirruped round in search of oats. Ideal for drawing.

Sunny

In the afternoon I had to go to Stogumber to fetch a chicken from Mrs Read. The Captain asked me to help him catch ponies in a field behind Woolston Moor so I met him there. It took some time — Spicy was easy to catch, but the brown mare as difficult as ever. In the end I took Spicy up a narrow bridle path and the Captain drove the mare up till she was firmly wedged against us, with no possibility of escape unless she jumped right over us.

October 29th. I had a card from a Miss Joseph, whom I met at Canon Yates' lectures. They are arranging another course at Holford but it is difficult for me to get there. Miss Joseph says that a Miss Hall would take me from St Audries if I would telephone her. So I asked Chris' father, the Williton station master, to telephone her for me which he kindly did.

I had a rush to get up the hill to St Audries by 2.15 as my train does not get in till 1.50. However, I did it and there was Miss Hall, a tall, good looking girl about my age. But she had a puncture and we had to crawl all the way in second gear, stopping at Kilve to pick up the Parson's wife.

The hut at Holford was packed by the time Canon Yates arrived. This course is on contemporary fiction, and his subject today was Arnold Bennett. I was very much interested; I have not read any of his novels but by the end of the lecture felt as if I had.

At the end a lady asked some questions in which — greatly daring — I joined and we had an interesting discussion on Beauty in the realistic novel.

Though the Canon lectures well, he is rather gushing and

sentimental; I did not care for being called his "dear young lady" in front of a large audience, nor for "how sweet of you to notice that". He seemed very pleased to see me and wished I could come each week. I should like to hear the next lecture as it is to be on Conrad — I really enjoy the lectures apart from the gush.

Mrs James invited me to have tea with her and a tall and beautiful woman with jade earrings was sympathetic about my difficulties with transport and asked if it would help if I lunched with her.

I hurried away after tea as I had planned to walk home over the hills.

The contrast between the crowded hut full of women chatting round the Canon and the lonely glen was striking; what did they know of beauty down there? I felt very superior as I climbed up the hill but as I got higher I did not feel superior at all — I felt very small.

It was still light, but evening was coming on, the sky already grey with mist veiling it. The air was cold and damp with a pungent smell of rotting leaves. I hurried up the wooded bridle path, oaks and beeches overhead and a carpet of dead leaves underfoot. When I came out on the turf track at the top to see the line on line, ridge on ridge of swelling grey hills I had to stop. Below me on the right were soft twiggy tree tops and beyond miles of country revealed by grey washes of light.

There are rows of huge beeches on this track, enormous columned giants, and the wind was singing in their branches like a great organ. I felt there was something living walking beside me — it was more than a feeling, it was a certainty. It was as if someone for whom you have been looking all your life has come and taken your hand. He is there and joy sings in your heart. I suddenly knew that I never need doubt, that it was true.

I went on almost running, the wind blowing me forward so that I jumped from tussock to tussock, saying "It's true, it's true". I did not know what I meant, only that I could have died then for joy.

Dusk fell quickly as I was crossing the high hill above Bicknoller Post. The colour left the bracken and mist scudded over the ridges excluding the light. It was dark, and at the Post I walked into a herd of ponies. They neighed with fright and galloped off, then stopped to look. A little foal no bigger than a dog ran along the top of Weacombe, whinnying with terror.

Weacombe seemed very long and very dark after the open hill. Sheep glimmered white on the sides and thorn trees loomed up unexpectedly, while beside me in the gully the brook rushed and roared. I hoped that every dark object would turn out to be a stag but it never did, and then I came to the pitchy dark of the larch wood and at last the cheerful light from our window.

A delicious late tea was ready and to my astonishment, this walk which in feeling had lasted a year had really taken less than an hour. I must have flown, for it was five miles up and down and a rough track all the way.

CHAPTER VI

October 30th — December 22nd, 1926

❧❧❧❧ ❧❧❧❧

*O*CTOBER *30th.* Winifred came for the week-end today. AVS had a letter from her mother in India recently, saying that she is taking her from school soon, and would AVS have her as a PG? This is splendid, as they get on well, and it will help to keep things going.

We cycled to Williton to shop, and in the evening went by the hill-path to fetch the second post from Bicknoller. Winifred chattered about school and Miss Webster the whole way — it does seem funny to be with someone who talks even more than I do!

There was the most glorious sunset. Clouds had massed in parallel lines in the West, those below fiery scarlet, with rays of pure gold piercing them. Above, they were deep purple edged with dazzling light, and higher still enormous indigo cumuli were piled in fantastic shapes.

The colour faded, and we watched the sun, a huge scarlet ball, sink through a gap. It was quiet as we stood there — Winifred silent for once — and we heard a man's voice, miles away, and the creak of a waggon, remote and drowsy in the calm.

There are always a great many birds by that path — pigeons, woodpeckers, tree creepers, stone and whin-chats, tits of every sort, and of course blackbirds and both the thrushes. I saw a pair of gold-crests recently.

November 2nd. I was allowed to go to the Opening Meet at St Audries this year, a long-standing promise as a reward for School Certificate, and invited Mr Wood and Karen. They came by train and I met them on the main road. Half Minehead seemed to be in the park and three of the Harrow boys. The little Archers looked very proud, one on a fat pony and the other astride a donkey. Mr Sweet Escott was on Swallow, and to my chagrin, told me that he had to leave at 12.30 and I could take the mare on if I liked. Of course, as the Woods were there, I had to refuse.

Mr Wood, who had said he would not know a soul, was continually hailed: "Hulloh Wood! Haven't seen you for an age!" He used to shoot here every year and had had many a day's sport in the good old days.

Hounds did not move off till noon but found at once and the woods around the park were soon ringing. The fox circled, and then crossed the main road to Staple. We cut up the quarry and joined the field above Weacombe. A rumour went round that hounds had chopped the fox in the plantation, but at any rate they lost him. After about half an hour it was decided to move on, and they found on the brow of Staple Plain. This one went to ground, and the next was lost in a flock of sheep. We saw the pack running well, in full cry, with the fox just ahead towards the little flock, and then they stopped, and though Charlie cast all round there was no sign of Reynard.

We sat down to wait till they found again but they careered away to the other side of the hills. After all the clamour was gone a huge stag came out of the combe. He seemed to be moving in a queer way, and Mr Wood, who had field glasses, said he had a broken leg.

We stayed on the hill till about three o'clock, seeing nothing more of the hunt, but enjoying the magnificent cloud effects. Ravenously hungry by then, we returned for a royal tea in our kitchen.

November 4th. Uncle Arthur has sent me some Bridge scorers, as we play regularly in the train now. This morning, as we were one short, a nice commercial traveller took a hand. I had brought a set of fox's teeth that I took from a skull years ago on the Brendons; he was so intrigued with them that I gave him three. A kind act I now regret, as I had the whole set.

A letter has come from Narney, asking us to wire to say if we can have her here for her holiday. I hope it will be fine, for the weather is fearfully stormy. An elm tree blew across the line last night which delayed the train and when it did come it stood in the station long enough for a whole hand of Bridge.

November 5th. Narney jumped from the train with "Hulloh, Kid!", tall and slim and pretty as ever. She has had her hair shingled and looks years younger. We walked home together, me wheeling her suit-case on my bicycle, and longing to see her face when we came in view of the cottage.

November 7th. Narney and I took a very stormy walk to Holford, sunshine alternating with drenching rain. At the top of Weacombe we paused to look back. For the moment the county was in brilliant light and we heard the church bells ringing for Matins. Three different chimes came clean and sweet, louder and fainter as the wind blew.

We argued heatedly most of the time about my future, Narney strongly disapproving of my going in for drawing; she hates "these ornamental professions!"

However, coming back we stopped quarrelling, and compared notes on our family, its sins and shortcomings. And then on to the never-failing hospital stories, some of which kept us in fits of laughter as we came down Staple Plain.

November 9th. I was asked to sleep with Mrs Evans Smith, as the Captain is away and she does not like being alone. We spent a gloriously cosy evening over a roaring fire, the lamp and a bag of sweets between us. After the gales yesterday it was a calm night — just as well, as we found the glass of the lantern broken, and had to water and inspect the ponies last thing by the light of the sitting-room candles in their silver sticks.

But in the small hours the gale rose again, and heavy rain woke me. I gave up all idea of going to school and helped feed the hens and goats, washed up and lit the fire. Mr Frost, coming in for cocoa, kindly drove me home through the deluge.

November 16. The weather continues to be frightful — I have not had a ride for three weeks. And I am tired of getting wet through day after day. A brighter state of affairs seems to be dawning though, as Dorothy Dalzell is at home again and has nice Sally Hall with her; they are hoping to get up a dance.

This afternoon there was a knock at our door and in came Dorothy, to invite me for tomorrow night. She had Sally in the car, so I went out, and after some hesitation they asked me how well I knew the Sweet Escotts. Being re-assured, they asked me to invite some of the boys to the dance, as they are short of men, and I was carried off to Bicknoller PO to telephone.

Mr Sweet Escott is difficult to understand on the 'phone; he splutters and shouts worse than in person. However, I did manage to make out that he was "Very sorry, but all the boys are working for an examination". On the way home it was decided to put off the dance and have the evening just for the three of us. Sally is going to teach me the Charleston.

*November 20th.*I practised the Charleston so energetically while dressing that AVS came up to tell me to stop, as the ceiling would not stand it.

I was in despair about my ride as it was again very wet, but 'Rain before seven, fine before eleven' came true. I rode a new pony named

Crackers, very fresh, and not needing a word to make him trot. Mr Frost, on Duncan, had rheumatism and was feeling cross, so it was not a lively ride as far as he was concerned. I did not mind, it was so lovely to be on a horse again.

We had five horses to dress when we got in, and it was raining again. I had half a mind to leave Crackers for Duddles, to pay him out for being cross. But it seemed too bad when he was really in pain. There is a great deal of excuse for him as he has suffered so much with his fractures — but I do hate moody boys!

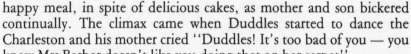

I rode Prudence in the afternoon, as fat as a pig and as scornful as ever, and jogged round Vellow, afterwards being invited to tea at the Frosts. Not a

Pudding

happy meal, in spite of delicious cakes, as mother and son bickered continually. The climax came when Duddles started to dance the Charleston and his mother cried "Duddles! It's too bad of you — you know Mrs Barber doesn't like you doing that on her carpet".

I was glad to leave, and uneasy at having no lights on my bicycle. Mr Frost assured me that the village Bobby is seldom seen, so I rode to the village for the letters. A large parcel had come and I had to walk resting it on the saddle. And well I did so, for halfway down the hill who should I meet but two luckless youths without lights, having their names taken by a very angry policeman!

November 21st. We expected Mother and Dicky today, as he is fetching her from Hardown. They came about 11 a.m. and went into ecstasies over the cottage.

AVS being busy cooking lunch, I took them up the combe. Dicky was greatly struck, as was evident by his constant "By Jove!" He loves the country so much that it seems a shame he should have to be a solicitor, stuck in a London office. However, now that he has a car he can get away; he says he has not spent a week-end in town since June.

Mother has been over-working in the garden and cannot climb hills as a result — she always strains her heart at Hardown. So she soon returned to the cottage; Dicky and I walked on to St Audries.

The Brown Mare

November 22nd. Directly after breakfast Dicky and I set off to Elworthy. Mrs Hayes was amazed and delighted at our early appearance, and presently in came Ned, his face glowing with pleasure. "Did you see the bullocks on Hill Road?" he asked. "I've got 'em there and ought to look them over today." We ran him up in the car, and he took the gun and the ferrets so that Dicky should "have a bit of sport". As Bill Tarr had wired the hill fields and caught seventy-five in one night it was feared there might be few rabbits left; Ned said he had had 600 already this year.

November 25th. Miss Ford, Miss Smith, and I had three gypsy women as companions in our carriage this morning. Miss Ford and I enjoyed them but Miss Smith was disgusted. Two were real gypsies — brown skin, black hair and eyes, gold rings and earings, and oily, yet harsh voices. The other was quite an ordinary girl; they called her Amy. She and the older woman had small babies wrapped in blankets whom they were dressing, un-dressing, or feeding throughout the entire journey.

The younger gypsy — evidently the older one's daughter — could not keep still. She jumped up and down, jigging her knees, whistled, and talked very fast, quite unintelligibly, though I understood a phrase now and then. Her laugh was like a rook's caw, and she smoked and took snuff alternately. We were given a history of all her clothes, beginning with "Me shift — I got that to Bampton" and ending with "Me lil' old jumper". I was thankful there were no men in the carriage, for we were given the most intimate details. I thought poor Miss Smith would never survive the list!

November 26th. Lady Trevelyan and her two daughters, from Nettlecombe Court, are kindly giving me lifts to and from Holford for the lectures. I met their car outside the station today, and sat behind with Lady T. and one daughter — the other had gone to Malta. They are very pleasant, affable people.

The lecture was excellent, on a group of Humourists. I howled with mirth at some of the quotations. We had O. Henry, W. W. Jacobs, Leacock, Chesterton, and Saki — I'm ashamed to say I know nothing of the last.

Afterwards the Canon came up to me for a talk about Samuel Butler apropos of Mother's book; he wants to come and see her at Highgate.

The drive back was lovely, particularly the bit of road where the Quantocks slope down to the Channel. Beyond the glowing autumn woods we saw the dim coastline, North Hill lying like a great lion. It was especially beautiful this evening, a pink glow in the sky and a blue mist veiling the furthest hills.

December 3rd. The Evans Smiths are again in the throes of theatricals. The Captain has written the play, and is to produce it for the Bicknoller British Legion. It is to be 'The Co-Pessimists' and the cast is to be dressed in Pierrot costume. The curtain is to rise on a moonlit scene with the troupe singing 'I want the moon'; it will be a wonderful sight — I long to see our neighbour Treble as a Pierrot!

Mrs Evans Smith is frantically cutting up white calico and vowing, as usual, that she will never get involved in theatricals again. The Captain spent the morning lying on the floor painting posters.

The hounds ran to and fro this afternoon. I heard them in full cry and ran out, to be greeted by Sir Dennis: "Which way?" – "Straight up the combe," I shouted, and he thanked me and galloped past, followed by the field. Later stragglers included the Kershaws, very cross; Peggy said they were having a beastly day — nothing but climbing up and down precipices!

Just at dusk Charlie and Taylor came up the lane with the pack, blowing the horn to collect any stray hounds, and then silence.

December 7th. My ride today was wholly occupied by errands in Stogumber, riding Filbert, the Captain on the brown gelding. I was sent to Miss Sully to pay her account, then to Goodings shop to buy Nice biscuits. We were hanging about for quite half an hour, what with a visit to Mrs Févre and Nurse. Then we had to go to the Knoll to borrow some theatrical things. However no one was at home but Joan Kershaw, who came and stood on one leg in the yard and kept us talking. The Captain was in one of his most absurd moods, which brightened the rest of the ride. He produced a false beard, put it on, and rode with hunched shoulders, legs and elbows out at angles, and assumed the most appalling squint. He was so funny that I could not protest for laughing.

Nearing home, I complained bitterly at having to live in London. The Captain was most sympathetic, and suggested a diet of chalk, which he assured me would make me look too ill to leave the country.

December 9th. Capt. Brandling has written to the Kemp Welch Art School at Bushey for me, as I feared my parents might enroll me at one in London if nothing was done. So I arrived for my lesson today in a great state of anticipation. "Oh, I've heard from Miss Kemp Welch," he said, as soon as we were settled. "Have you?" said I with a beating heart. "And I'm afraid she herself gave up the school last year. However, her secretary, Miss Frobisher, still keeps it on, and Wheelwright, who was at Herkomer's in my day, comes to take classes for horse-painting twice a week''. This seemed promising and we proceeded to discuss it. Mr B. thought it ideal — out of London, so a good light, a small school, which is what the occulist advised, and good teaching. And a pleasant school, assuming no great alteration since last year. I needed no urging when he strongly advised me to go.

December 10th. It being the last dancing class of the term, we were each allowed to bring a friend, and Karen came as mine, to the Wellington Hotel. I was amazed at her prowess at the Charleston — she did it beautifully — I find it more difficult. We polkad and gallopped till I nearly dropped, and then went through Sir Roger twice.

Karen Wood

Tea and the genial company at the Woods revived me. Mr Wood had just got in from hunting and said they had killed three deer. Karen and I caught the 6.45 train and walked to Weacombe through pitchy darkness.

After that, and all the dancing, neither of us 'needed rocking' and were asleep as soon as our heads were on our pillows.

December 14th. I thought I had never seen anything more lovely than the top of the hills today, a radiant one of white frost and pale sky. I rode Filbert; he went very well up to Bicknoller Post. The sun was melting the hoar-frost up there and sheep were grazing the heather, each in a halo of steam. Down below the mists were dissolving; everything seemed fresh and as if no one had set foot up there before.

We trotted briskly from the Post to the 'blasted pine' and then walked down the lane to Staple. I rode up to "Hulloh!" the cottage, AVS looked out to wave, then with a splash I crossed the stream and went by the hill path to Bicknoller.

In the afternoon, again on Filbert, I met Duddles riding a brown pony and leading his old Dobin. He asked if I were in a hurry, and if not, if I would lead his horse as the brown would not go, leading. So I had the pleasure of an extra ride, and of leading, which I like. As it turned out, it was exciting — Filbert took fright at something near Stogumber station, and barged past a large waggon lumbering up the hill.

We got past it and the two cart horses somehow, and went on at a fine gallop, Dobin valiantly coming along too.

Several women walking up from the train hurriedly got into the ditch, evidently thinking it a case of 'run away horse'. However, old Filbert's bark is always worse than his bite and he soon calmed down. The next time he galloped the brown pony felt gay too, and executed two enormous bucks. These took Mr Frost by surprise and he nearly came off — but not so nearly as he afterwards made out.

December 17th. I made a round of visits today, speeding off to Stogumber soon after breakfast. Dull as Ashpier is to climb, it is very nice to turn round and see the roofs of Stogumber shelving up below, crowned with the fine Church tower and backed by the long line of the Quantocks.

Once on top it was an easy spin down to Elworthy, where I stayed a little while talking to the Hayes and learning of the latest deaths.

From there I visited dear Mrs Ware, who was worshipping a fine baby, Mrs Rutts' grand-child. He is a beautiful, fat child now and it is hard to believe that his life was despaired of not long ago.

At the Middletons I had a great deal to hear, a warm welcome, and hearty goodbye kisses. Hartrow came next, and I stayed to lunch. I met Mr Sweet Escott in the drive: "Have you seen my stables?" "Yes, often — why?" "Oh, come along, come along," and he marched me off. The stables had been completely done up; painted and repaired, and now have four spacious loose-boxes instead of the old stalls, while — marvel of marvels — water and electric light are laid on.

Everyone was at lunch, including Guy — so nice! And all so sorry that I am leaving. Mr Sweet Escott said he would have something for me to ride every holiday, and his wife and her sister kissed me goodbye.

December 19th. The Hayes family came to tea today, arriving about five in a hired car. Mrs Hayes brought a pot of her delicious butter and a bowl of very thick clotted cream. Her dairy is exceptionally good, she says, for the time of the year. Everyone talked and laughed throughout tea except Gordon, who like a sensible boy, stuffed solidly. He had something of everything, and at last sat back, sighing with content, saying he "Couldn't eat no more, thank'ee, Miss Anne."

December 20th. I went to Minehead for the last time today, taking a small remembrance present for Miss Ford. It was a book of the proofs for one of Father's translations of Dumas Pére, neatly bound. I knew she liked Dumas, and sure enough, she was most appreciative.

There are so many good-byes now, and I hate them! I had to bid farewell to our Bridge four, and then to everyone at school.

After lunch I hurriedly finished my gardening as I want to leave it tidy; I have planted a great many bulbs. Also the Sweet Escotts were coming to tea.

They arrived with Miss Robertson and were soon seated in the parlour in a buzz of conversation. "What a *charming* view!" "Anna, is not this an exquisite situation?" "My dear, I think you are most fortunate." One of the many reasons for loving Mrs Sweet Escott and her sister is that they talk in low, sweet voices, straight out of Jane Austen.

Meanwhile I was talking to Mr Escott in the window and he said "Look here, can you manage a meet at Clatworthy tomorrow? You can have Swallow if you like". And tomorrow is my birthday too!

I was so excited that it was difficult to think of anything else; however, I took Mr Sweet Escott out to the garden and showed him round.

In the evening I set out for Bicknoller, for the dress rehearsal of 'The Co-Pessimists'. A full moon was rising and her light fell ahead of me in pools of silver, whereas I walked in inky blackness. Then she sailed up behind the jet-black pines and I saw her full globe against the serene blue sky.

Chinks of yellow light shone from the barn door, and there were sounds of mirth within. I pushed open the door to find sundry villagers around a screen, through which shone a bright light. "Is that you, Anne?" came the Captain's voice: "For God's sake stay outside the screen — it's our dressing-room".

Mrs Evans Smith was at the piano, and soon began to thump it till the stage shook. At last a frantic voice shouted "Barber! Barber — the curtain! Draw the curtain!" The curtain shook, drew back, stuck, jerked, and finally parted, revealing — oh, lovely sight — a starry sky and shining silver moon. A soulful wheeze proceeded from the piano, and the troupe of Pierrots made its entry.

They sang their sorrowful 'Want the Moon' and then proceeded to more cheerful solos. The best item was a quartette: 'We are the filberts that grow in Mayfair', sung with top hats over their skull caps, eye-glasses and carrying canes. Another in the same vein was the Captain's 'I did feel Frightfully Ass'.

Treble and another then came on in smocks as old gaffers watching an imaginary cricket match, which they did in broad dialect. I was amazed at Treble, in life a typical farm labourer, bowed and stumpy. Not only was he excellent as the Gaffer, which he did to perfection, but he was a wonderful pierrot, singing and dancing as lively as a cricket.

We then saw the scene written by the Captain. He was an Italian organ-grinder, whose monkey had been assassinated, very well disguised with curling moustaches and a truly wonderful organ.

His companions wore large slouch hats and blankets; they all had blood-stained stillettos and ate yards of spaghetti out of a sack.

Mrs Dalzell who was watching with me and I laughed till we wept. It was too funny to describe. I enjoyed the whole rehearsal and thought it most successful.

December 21st. My birthday morning! I rushed to the window as soon as I woke — the day was grey and windy, but with no trace of rain.

There was nothing from my family among my post, at which I felt a little hurt. But I forgot this as I hurriedly dressed to ride, and swallowed down as much breakfast as I could — it seemed to stick in my throat.

Having pocketed some sandwiches I rushed off to Stogumber where the Hartrow stable-boy was to meet me with Swallow. But there was no sign of them so I went in to talk to Mrs Read. It seemed an age before I heard horses' hoofs.

Swallow was far too fresh, cantering up Ashpier and galloping along the top road. At one point I lost my stirrups and only managed to cling on by sheer luck. If she were like this on the way to the meet what would she be with hounds running? Terror assailed me, and I had half a mind to turn in at Hartrow, but the humiliation of confessing that I could not hold Swallow prevented me.

I rode down Truckwell Lane; she went very nicely downhill and my courage revived. We cantered up to Brompton Ralph and she was much more manageable. I came to the conclusion that she had had a good feed of oats for breakfast and that the effects were just wearing off.

It seemed a long way to Clatworthy and I knew I should be late for the meet. At the cross roads on the Brendons I came up with Harry Sweet Escott and rode on with him. Some cars stood outside Clatworthy Church and there were numerous small boys, but no sign of the hunt. However, Mr Harry knew where it would be, so we rode down the valley to where some grooms with second horses were waiting under a beech wood.

From them we learnt that hounds were drawing a covert high above, so we rode up a very steep hill and found them opposite, across a little valley. Soon after, they found, and in full cry came streaming across our field. We gave rein and galloped after them, the huntsmen and field behind us. All trace of fear vanished; I sat tight and felt Swallow opening up her speed. Her ears cocked, and snorting for joy, she went like the wind. Mr Harry's horse was slower; I passed him, and followed the hounds up a steep path through the woods.

We were soon out of the trees and galloping over a level meadow;

there then came another climb up the further side of the valley. No one could gallop here; we had a zigzag up, and several horses began to steam. A chestnut mare with a pronounced ewe-neck made a fearful noise with her broken wind. Her rider, a fat, smiling fellow, remarked on this with great joviality to anyone within ear-shot. I had not heard a real roarer before.

We hung about on the hill-top for some time and the horses ceased panting. Nothing seemed likely to happen, so we descended to the meadow again. Swallow and I took it rather slowly, so were behind by the time we reached the level. She did not care for this and began to gallop as if the devil were at her heels. In less than a minute we were at the end of the field, scattering some boys left and right. "Coo, can't 'er ride!" called one, to my delight! So we came up to the rest, waiting in a lane below the wood.

We soon realised that the fox had gone to ground. Mr Frank Hancock — Sir Dennis was not out today — was on foot among the pack and we waited while he poked about. But it was a main earth and hopeless to think of digging, so we moved off.

A spinney was unsuccessfully drawn and hounds slowly quartered the steep hill-side. We stayed on top and I could look at the view. Below us in the valley, with its green fields and stream, was a nice farm with its barns and ricks. Beyond, a hill closed in the valley, all bracken and woods. To the north, Clatworthy church tower rose square and white on its knoll, above it ridge upon ridge of wild hills rising to the highest point of the Brendons. And against this stood the cheerful group of horsemen with their pink coats, glossy black hats and shining horses, bay, brown, chestnut and grey, gossiping as they waited.

Mr Harry stayed with one group and I tried to keep near, as I did not want to get lost. The party consisted of Major Rose, a pretty, dashing girl with her young husband, and a blonde, older woman riding side-saddle, who chattered incessantly and tried to be kittenish.

Just as I was growing rather bored, and longed for another burst, hounds found and a glorious peal went ringing through the woods. Mr Harry was now nowhere to be seen so I went on with people I was with, up a narrow path where hazel bushes scraped our heads, into a top field. Here were many rabbit holes, and had it not been

Riding side-saddle

for a kindly warning from Sir Harry Mallet I should have galloped right into them.

78

It was not long before a wild shriek came from a hill top and someone exclaimed "There he goes!" A little red dot was hurrying along with the hounds close behind. We turned and galloped back down the wood and along a steep field — so steep that we used the bed of a stream for foot-hold — over a ditch and some hurdles and into the wood beyond.

We came up just too late for the kill. Mr Hancock came out of a gap in the hedge, followed by Charlie with the hounds flowing round him, and the more fortunate followers who had stayed on the right side of the valley. Among those was Mr Harry, of whom I asked the time.

It was half past two, so remembering my birthday tea, I thought I had best make for home. Mr Harry gave me directions, telling me to strike across the fields and make for Raleigh's Cross.

Fortunately I came up with a groom going the same way, or I might have wandered about those fields all night, each one being exactly the same as the last. We ambled slowly along, my companion remarking that it was lucky Swallow was so good mannered, as no one could hold her when she had a mind to go!

I was tired and stiff when I dismounted at Hartrow, and ran in to tell of my return. But I only saw Mrs Sweet Escott, to whom I tried to express my delight at having actually been hunting on my own.

There was time to change before my party, to which Mrs Evans Smith and Mr Frost arrived; the Captain had to send his apologies. We had a magnificent iced cake with the appropriate greetings and a white horse on top, lots of other good things — and crackers.

Sitting around the fire I recounted all my adventures and Mr Frost told me who all the people were. The blonde kittenish woman runs a Nursing Home in Minehead.

About eight Guy came in for coffee and consumed large portions of my cake. He is very entertaining and is always full of local news so it is nice to see more of him again — he was in and out so much at Elworthy.

December 22nd. The last day dawned clear and bright, and the postman brought me a birthday present from Mother, who is in bed with a bad cold. She will try to meet my train tomorrow. From her letter I can see that we are in for a difficult Christmas, as Miss Love is away and the temporary cook cannot come. Housework is horrid in that great dreary house! The only gleam of light is that Uncle Arthur will be there.

I went to the stables and went out with Mr Frost, the last ride together as it were. We had bright sunshine the whole way so it was impossible to feel gloomy. From Weacombe we rode to Quantock

Moor and amused ourselves by jumping over and over a bank. Filbert was feeling merry and it was quite hard to hold him. It was an enjoyable ride, the bracken and heather such a lovely colour in the sunshine.

While I was receiving instructions from Mrs Evans Smith as to errands she wanted done, the Captain came bursting in: "Ducky, I've made our fortunes — I've been to an auction at Williton and bought up all the old china and glass". "Cecil! You *haven't*!" wailed his wife. "And I need a new hat so badly! Now I suppose you have spent all our cash." — "No I haven't, — only £30," said the Captain. "We'll sell it for three times that amount — you'll see."

He continued in this strain, enlarging on the value of his purchases till we realised he had in all probability spent about five shillings. Presently Mrs Dalzell came in to hear about the auction, and was so thrilled that the Captain said he would drive her there. They bustled about getting ready and meanwhile Duddles looked in to say goodbye to me. He wrung my hand hard and wished me good luck; I felt much affected.

After a melancholy farewell to the Captain it was rather a relief to find that Mrs Evans Smith had gone with him, when I returned from my errands — I felt I had said quite enough goodbyes. Each of these last days has seemed better than ever — only more laden with the sadness of leaving. I have dreaded going to bed, knowing that I should lie staring at the dark in a sort of panic — I cannot face up to London! It has been a relief to cry myself to sleep.

I shan't write any more in this diary — I shall be too busy, going out to Bushey every day, and I would rather leave it as a record of these last happy, happy years. If someday it helps me to remember it all, it will not have been written in vain.

FINIS

Far away are those years. All the glossy horses — Swallow and Conga, gentle Mildmay, the evil brown mare, and naughty James Pigg — have long since fed the hounds

Arthur Garnett was drowned in 1927, swimming in a rough sea with Robert off the treacherous shingle below Gold Cap. Life for Elizabeth, Dicky, and Anne was never the same without him.

Nearly all the people Anne wrote of are, alas, dead and gone. The valley where she galloped on that memorable birthday is no more, its farm, ricks, and barns fathoms deep in Clatworthy Reservoir. Gone are the carts with their shafts in the air, the cocks, hens, and pigs in farm-yards, and the creek of waggon wheels in the lanes.

AVS remained at the Weacombe cottage seven years. By that time her high standards had exhausted the capabilities of all available 'dailies' and she took to lodgings once more. These she changed so frequently that a special book was needed for her addresses. She lived to her ninety-third year.

Anne had the good sense to marry a West Somerset man, Frank Lee Michell, brother to Constance who used to ride with Captain Evans Smith. They were married in 1930, at Whitchurch Canonicorium, the Reverend Herbert Sweet Escott officiating; had two daughters, and lived happily ever after.

Also by Anne Garnett:

CAUGHT FROM TIME: A Country Diary of the 1920s

The first part of Anne Garnett's two-volume West Somerset diary, concluded by *Fields of Young Corn.*
'Freshness and naturalness shine out of her pages and it is a delightful and tranquil book' *The Catholic Herald*
'Original and entertaining impressions of country life in the '20s' *Cambridge Evening News*
'Sensitive notes on the changing seasons; on her friendships with local farmers, vivid accounts of memorable events such as the funeral of old Isaac Hayes . . . In all, this makes delightful nostalgic reading' Victor Bonham Carter, *The Exmoor Review*
'The perfect bedside book' *Western Morning News*
'A joy to read' *This England*
'Some charming colour sketches' *The Field*
Cover, line and water-colour drawings by the author, and photographs. 132pp £10.95

AND THEN THERE WAS ONE *by* Joyce Dennys

Joyce Dennys has written her lively memoir with perception and depth, and illustrated it by distinctive line drawings that are reminiscent of her cartoons for the *Weekly Sketch* and *Punch*. The daughter of an Indian Army Officer who seldom came home to his wife and family, and one of a large number of brothers, one sister, and cousins, she conveys with humour and charm the spartan yet secure world of her Victorian-Edwardian childhood.
'A most engaging account of her early life. Warmly recommended'
The London Standard
'This is a delightful "childhood" book. Significant in content right through, summing up events with a humorous precision. A crisply-told story.' *Catholic Herald*
'Gem of a book' *Church Times*
Line drawings by the author and photographs. 104 pp. Sewn pbk. £2.99